A2 Biology
UNIT 6

AQA

Specification A

Module 6: Physiology and the Environment

Steve Potter

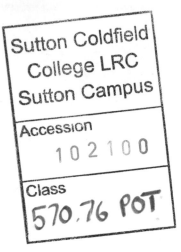
Philip Allan Updates
Market Place
Deddington
Oxfordshire
OX15 0SE

tel: 01869 338652
fax: 01869 337590
e-mail: sales@philipallan.co.uk
www.philipallan.co.uk

© Philip Allan Updates 2001

ISBN 0 86003 489 5

This Guide has been written specifically to support students preparing for the AQA Specification A A2 Biology Unit 6 examination. The content has been neither approved nor endorsed by AQA and remains the sole responsibility of the author.

Printed by Information Press, Eynsham, Oxford

P00059

Contents

Introduction

■ ■ ■

Content Guidance

■ ■ ■

Questions and Answers

Introduction

About this guide

This guide is written to help you to prepare for the Unit 6 examination of the AQA Biology Specification A. Unit 6 examines the content of **Module 6: Physiology and the Environment**, and forms part of the A2 assessment.

This Introduction provides guidance on revision, together with advice on approaching the examination itself.

The Content Guidance section gives a point-by-point description of all the facts you need to know and concepts you need to understand for Module 6. Although each fact and concept is explained where necessary, you must be prepared to use other resources in your preparation.

The Question and Answer section shows you the sort of questions you can expect in the unit test. It would be impossible to give examples of every kind of question in one book, but these should give you a flavour of what to expect. Each question has been attempted by two candidates, Candidate A and Candidate B. Their answers, along with the examiner's comments, should help you to see what you need to do to score a good mark — and how you can easily *not* score a mark even though you probably understand the biology.

Preparing for the Unit 6 test

Preparation for examinations is a very personal thing. Different people prepare, equally successfully, in very different ways. The key is being totally honest about what actually *works* for *you*. This is *not* necessarily the same as the style you would like to adopt. It is no use preparing to a background of rock music if this distracts you.

Whatever your style, you must have a plan. Sitting down the night before the examination with a file full of notes and a textbook does not constitute a revision plan — it is just desperation — and you must not expect a great deal from it. Whatever your personal style, there are a number of things you *must* do and a number of other things you *could* do.

Things you *must* do

- Leave yourself enough time to cover *all* the material. This is especially important for the Unit 6 test, as it not only covers the Module 6 content, but also includes **synoptic** questions based on principles and concepts from other modules.
- Make sure that you actually *have* all the material to hand (use this book as a basis).
- Identify weaknesses early in your preparation so that you have time to address them.

- Make sure that you do something about these weaknesses.
- Familiarise yourself with the terminology used in examination questions (see below).

Things you *could* do to help you learn

- Write a precis of portions of your notes, including all the relevant key points.
- Produce unlabelled diagrams of relevant structures, photocopy them and practise labelling them.
- Practise creating flow charts that summarise processes.
- Write a precis of your notes which includes all the key points.
- Write key points on postcards (carry them round with you for a quick revise during a coffee break!).
- Discuss a topic with a friend also studying the same course.
- Try to explain a topic to someone *not* on the course.
- Practise examination questions on the topic.

Approaching the unit test

Terms used in examination questions

You will be asked precise questions in the examinations, so you can save a lot of valuable time as well as ensuring you score as many marks as possible by knowing what is expected. Terms most commonly used are explained below.

Describe
This means exactly what it says — 'tell me about...' — and you should not need to explain why.

Explain
Here you must give biological reasons for *why* or *how* something is happening.

Complete
You must finish off a diagram, graph, flow chart or table.

Draw/plot
This means that you must construct some type of graph. For this, make sure that:
- you choose a scale that makes good use of the graph paper (if a scale is not given) and does not leave all the plots tucked away in one corner
- plot an appropriate type of graph — if both variables are continuous variables, then a line graph is usually the most appropriate; if one is a discrete variable, then a bar chart is appropriate
- plot carefully using a sharp pencil and draw lines accurately

From the...
This means that you must use only information in the diagram/graph/photograph or other forms of data.

Name

This asks you to give the name of a structure/molecule/organism etc.

Suggest

This means 'give a plausible biological explanation for' — it is often used when testing understanding of concepts in an unfamiliar situation.

Compare

In this case you have to give similarities *and* differences between...

Calculate

This means add, subtract, multiply, divide (do some kind of sum!) and show how you got your answer — *always show your working!*

When you finally open the test paper, it can be quite a stressful moment. You may not recognise the diagram or graph used in question 1. It can be quite demoralising to attempt a question at the start of an examination if you are not feeling very confident about it. So:

- *do not* begin to write as soon as you open the paper
- *do not* answer question 1 first, just because it is printed first (the examiner did not sequence the questions with your particular favourites in mind)
- *do* scan *all* the questions before you begin to answer any
- *do* identify those questions about which you feel most confident
- *do answer first* those questions about which you feel most confident regardless of order in the paper
- *do read the question carefully* — if you are asked to explain, then explain, don't just describe
- *do* take notice of the mark allocation and don't supply the examiner with all your knowledge of osmosis if there is only 1 mark allocated (similarly, you will have to come up with four ideas if 4 marks are allocated)
- *do* try to stick to the point in your answer (it is easy to stray into related areas that will not score marks and will use up valuable time)
- *do* take care with
  - drawings — you will not be asked to produce complex diagrams, but those you do produce must resemble the subject
  - labelling — label lines *must touch* the part you are required to identify; if they stop short or pass through the part, you will lose marks
  - graphs — draw *small* points if you are asked to plot a graph and join the plots with ruled lines or, if specifically asked for, a line or smooth curve of best fit through all the plots
- *do try* to answer *all* the questions

Content
Guidance

This section is a guide to the content of **Module 6: Physiology and the Environment**. The main areas of this module are:

- Transpiration
- The conflict between gas exchange and regulating water loss
- The transport of respiratory gases in mammals
- Digestion and absorption in mammals
- Diet, digestion and life histories
- Receptors in animals
- Transmission of information through the nervous system
- Integration and control by nerves and hormones
- Homeostasis

You should think of this section as a 'translation' of the specification from 'examiner speak' into more user-friendly language. At the same time I have tried to be very precise in describing exactly what is required of you.

Key facts you must know

These are exactly what you might think: a summary of all the basic knowledge that you must be able to recall. All the actual knowledge has been broken down into a number of small facts that you must learn. This means that the list of 'Key facts' for some topics is quite long. However, this approach makes quite clear *everything* you need to know about the topic.

Key concepts you must understand

Whereas you can learn facts, you must *understand* these ideas or concepts. You can know the actual words that describe a concept like mitosis, or DNA replication, but you will not be able to use this information unless you really understand what is going on. I have given brief explanations of all the major concepts, but you must be prepared to refer to your notes and textbooks or ask your teacher for a fuller explanation.

What the examiners will expect you to be able to do

In this part, I have tried to give you an insight into the minds of the examiners who will set and mark your examination papers. Obviously, they may ask you to recall any of the basic knowledge or explain any of the key concepts; but they may well do more than that. Examiners think up questions where the concepts you understand are in a different setting or context from the one(s) you are familiar with. I have tried, in this section, to prepare you for the sorts of questions they might ask. This can never be exhaustive, but it will give you a good idea of what can be asked of you. Bear in mind that examiners will often set individual questions that involve knowledge and understanding of more than one section. The sample questions in the Question and Answer section of this book will help you to practise this skill.

After most topics there is a short paragraph marked 'Synoptic links'. While not crucial to the understanding of any of the biology, this should give you some idea of how the biology you are learning will be related to other topics that you may meet in other modules.

Transpiration

Water movement through a plant

Key concepts you must understand

Water moves through a plant in the following ways:

- it moves from one living cell to another (across the roots and leaf) down a water potential gradient, by **osmosis**
- it moves through the xylem from root to leaf because of a combination of **physical forces**:
  - **root pressure** (a physical push)
  - **capillarity** (a process by which water 'creeps' up very narrow tubes)
  - **tension** (negative pressure) due to evaporation of water from the leaves (a pull)
- it **diffuses** down a water potential gradient from the air spaces of the spongy mesophyll of the leaf, through open stomata and into the atmosphere

Absorption by the roots and transfer to root xylem

Water enters the root epidermal cells, particularly the root hair cells, by osmosis down a water potential gradient. A water potential gradient exists across the root: the epidermal cells have a higher (less negative) water potential than cells in the centre of the root. Therefore, water moves towards the centre of the root where the xylem is found.

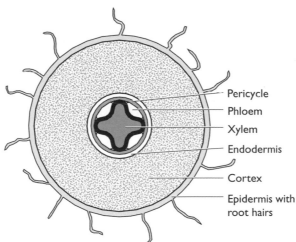

- Pericycle
- Phloem
- Xylem
- Endodermis
- Cortex
- Epidermis with root hairs

There are two main pathways by which water moves through the root:

- the **symplast** pathway — in this pathway, water moves through the walls, membranes and cytoplasm of the cells
- the **apoplast** pathway — in this pathway, water moves only through the cell walls and intercellular spaces.

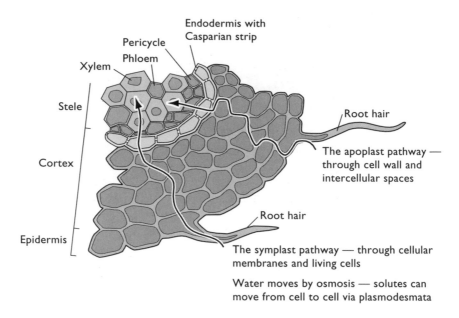

The cells of the endodermis have a layer of suberin (a fatty substance) called the **Casparian strip** in their walls. This acts as an apoplast block, preventing water from moving through the cell walls of the endodermal cells.

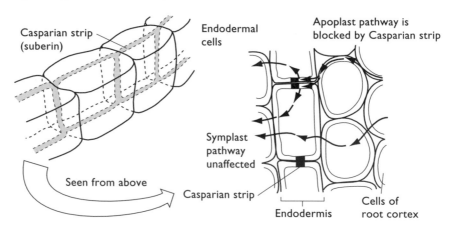

As more and more water enters the xylem in the centre of the root, it creates a pressure which forces the water up the xylem. This root pressure is one of the physical forces responsible for moving water up the xylem in roots and stems.

Loss from the leaves and transfer from the leaf xylem

A water potential gradient exists from the xylem in the leaf ($\Psi \approx -0.5$ MPa) to the leaf cells ($\Psi \approx -1.5$ MPa) to the air spaces ($\Psi \approx -10$ MPa) and finally to the atmosphere ($\Psi \approx -13$ to -120 MPa). When the guard cells open the stomata, water moves down this water potential gradient.

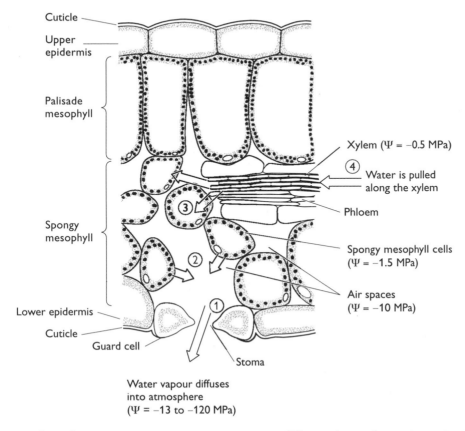

Cuticle

Upper epidermis

Palisade mesophyll

Xylem (Ψ = −0.5 MPa)

④ Water is pulled along the xylem

Phloem

Spongy mesophyll

Spongy mesophyll cells (Ψ = −1.5 MPa)

Air spaces (Ψ = −10 MPa)

Lower epidermis

Cuticle

Guard cell

Stoma

Water vapour diffuses into atmosphere (Ψ = −13 to −120 MPa)

(1) When the stomata are open, water vapour diffuses down the water potential (concentration) gradient from the air spaces into the atmosphere.

(2) More water evaporates from the surface of the spongy mesophyll cells into the air spaces, making the water potential of these cells more negative.

(3) Water passes, by osmosis, either from a neighbouring mesophyll cell or from a xylem vessel.

(4) The loss of water from the xylem creates a negative pressure or **tension** in the xylem and the water is pulled along.

All of these processes are dependent on the stomata being open. Transpiration ceases when the stomata are closed (except for a little **cuticular transpiration**, in which some water is lost through the waxy cuticle).

The currently favoured hypothesis of the regulation of stomatal opening and closing is the potassium ion pump hypothesis. According to this hypothesis, light activates a potassium pump that moves potassium ions into guard cells from neighbouring epidermal cells. This increase in concentration of potassium ions in the guard cells decreases (makes more negative) their water potential and so they take in water by osmosis. This causes the cells to swell, and because of the alignment of the cellulose fibrils in their cell walls, they become more curved in shape and open the stoma.

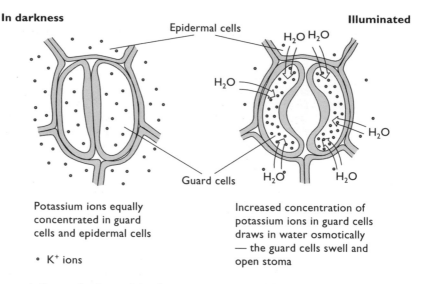

In darkness

Epidermal cells

Illuminated

H_2O H_2O

H_2O

H_2O

Guard cells

H_2O

H_2O

Potassium ions equally
concentrated in guard
cells and epidermal cells

• K^+ ions

Increased concentration of
potassium ions in guard cells
draws in water osmotically
— the guard cells swell and
open stoma

Movement through the xylem in stem, roots and leaves

Water moves up the stems in the xylem vessels, which form continuous narrow tubes from roots to leaves.

Transverse section of a young plant stem

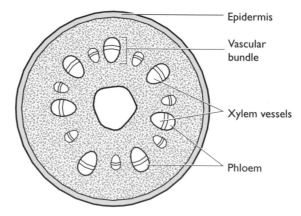

Epidermis

Vascular
bundle

Xylem vessels

Phloem

The position of the xylem in stems allows the stems to withstand the bending stresses to which they are subjected.

Water potential gradients move water from the soil to the xylem in the roots and from the xylem in the leaves to the atmosphere. However, there is no water potential gradient through the xylem. From the roots to the leaves, the water potential in the xylem is almost unchanged. Water moves through the xylem because of physical, rather than chemical, forces.

Possible explanations for the movement of water must account for water being pushed/pulled to heights of more than 30 metres.

Root pressure

As water enters the xylem in the roots by osmosis, it pushes water already present upwards.

Evidence in favour	Evidence against
Guttation — droplets of liquid water are sometimes seen at the edges of the leaves of small plants (this must be being forced out — normally only water vapour is lost) Water is pushed out of the cut ends of stems if the root system is still intact	Experimental measures of the force due to root pressure suggest that it is sufficient only to force water to a height of 4–5 metres up a stem

Root pressure alone is therefore insufficient to explain transpiration in large trees.

Capillarity

The continuous xylem vessels act like narrow capillary tubes. Water molecules adhere to the surfaces of the tubes and creep up the tube, pulling more water molecules with them.

Evidence in favour	Evidence against
Water does rise several metres up very narrow capillary tubes	Water can only move 1–2 metres up a tube that has the same diameter as a xylem vessel

The cohesion–tension theory driven by evaporation from the leaves

Evaporation from the spongy mesophyll cells and diffusion into the atmosphere draws water from the xylem in leaves by osmosis. This creates a negative pressure or tension on the water, pulling it upwards. Cohesive forces between water molecules in the xylem are strong enough to resist the tension. A column of water is pulled upwards through the xylem vessels.

Evidence in favour	Evidence against
When stomata open in the morning, water movement begins in the leaves, then in the stems The tension measured in water in the xylem vessels is great enough to lift a column of water well over 30 metres The cohesive forces are strong enough to resist the tension (so the water can move as a continuous column without 'breaking')	There is no significant evidence against this theory

The cohesion–tension theory, driven by evaporation from the leaves, is the currently accepted explanation of transpiration.

Factors affecting the rate of transpiration

The driving force for transpiration is the diffusion of water vapour through the stomata, followed by the evaporation of water from the surfaces of spongy mesophyll cells. Any factor that increases loss of water vapour by diffusion will increase evaporation and therefore increase the rate of transpiration. These factors can be grouped into two categories:

- those that affect the water potential gradient between the air spaces in the spongy mesophyll and the atmosphere
- those that affect the total stomatal aperture (effectively, this represents the surface area available for diffusion)

Factors affecting the water potential gradient include:

- atmospheric humidity. A high concentration of water vapour in the atmosphere will increase the water potential of the atmosphere (make it less negative). This will reduce the water potential gradient (concentration gradient of water vapour) between air spaces in the leaf and the atmosphere. The rate of transpiration will be reduced.
- atmospheric temperature. When temperature increases, the water vapour molecules have more kinetic energy; they move faster away from the stomata as they escape. This decreases the water potential of the atmosphere (makes it more negative) and so increases the water potential gradient (concentration gradient of water vapour) between air spaces and the atmosphere. The rate of transpiration increases.
- wind. Wind moves water vapour away from the stomata as they escape. This decreases the water potential of the atmosphere and increases the water potential gradient. The rate of transpiration increases.

Tip Anybody knows that clothes dry best on a warm, dry, windy day. All these factors move water vapour molecules away from the evaporating surface and increase the concentration gradient so that diffusion of vapour molecules increases.

Factors affecting total stomatal aperture include:

- number of stomata. Clearly, the more stomata there are in a given area of leaf epidermis, the greater the total aperture and the greater the rate of transpiration.
- light intensity. Light intensity drives the potassium pump which opens and closes each stoma, so affecting the total aperture. A rise in light intensity opens stomata, increasing the total aperture and so increasing the rate of transpiration.
- concentration of carbon dioxide *in the air spaces in the leaf* (atmospheric concentration varies very little). A low concentration of carbon dioxide in the air spaces limits the rate of photosynthesis and initiates the potassium pump mechanism which opens the stomata.

Measuring the rate of transpiration

There are two basic types of potometer:

- the bubble potometer, which measures the rate of water uptake by a plant by timing how quickly a bubble in a column of water moves a certain distance along capillary tubing of known diameter

• the mass potometer, which measures the water lost from a plant by measuring the change in mass over a period of time

The bubble potometer

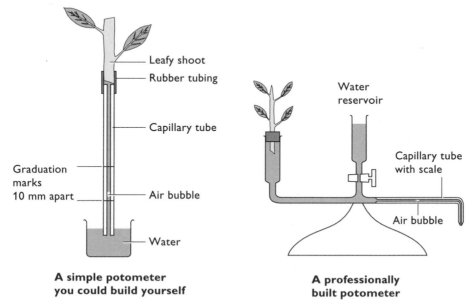

A simple potometer you could build yourself

A professionally built potometer

In both the designs shown, the rate of transpiration is measured by timing how long it takes for a bubble of air to move a set distance in mm.

The volume of water taken in can then be calculated (if the diameter of the capillary tubing is known) from the formula

$$volume = \pi r^2 l$$

where r = radius of capillary tubing ($\frac{1}{2}$ diameter) and l = distance moved by bubble.

Since the time for this volume of water to be taken in is known, the rate of water uptake per hour can be calculated.

The leafy shoot should be placed in the apparatus under water so that no unwanted air bubbles are introduced. The first design is easier to assemble and cheaper, but repeat readings are difficult to obtain as the apparatus must be re-assembled each time. The second apparatus is more costly and also slightly more difficult to assemble, but does allow repeat readings to be taken. After each reading, more water can be run into the apparatus from the reservoir, pushing the air bubble back to the end of the capillary tube, ready for another reading to be taken.

Both versions measure water uptake, which is assumed to be directly related to water loss by transpiration.

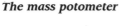

The mass potometer

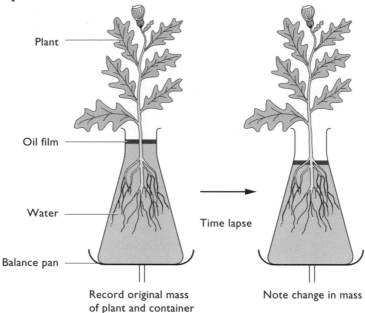

This apparatus does actually measure the amount of water lost, rather than the amount taken up. However, its accuracy is limited by the accuracy of the balance used to measure the mass. The assumption in this apparatus is that water loss from the plant accounts for the entire loss in mass. Some loss in mass could be due to losses through the oil film.

Xerophytes

Key facts you must know

Xerophytes are plants that live where water is in short supply. Plants living in arid conditions must either absorb as much water as possible when it is available, lose as little water as possible through transpiration, or do both.

Key concepts you must understand

Adaptations shown by xerophytes include:
- extensive root systems to absorb as much water as possible, quickly, when it rains
- reduced leaf area to minimise water loss (the spines of cacti are leaves)
- stems that are capable of:
  — photosynthesis (to compensate for the reduced photosynthesis by small leaves)
  — water storage

- sunken stomata, which lose less water because a high concentration of water vapour accumulates in the 'pits' and reduces the water potential gradient
- epidermal hairs, which also maintain a high concentration of water vapour near to the stomata
- a specialised type of photosynthesis (called CAM photosynthesis) in which the plants only absorb carbon dioxide from the atmosphere at night (so minimising stomatal opening in the extreme heat of the day)

What the examiners will expect you to be able to do

- Recall any of the key facts.
- Explain any of the key concepts.
- Interpret data on water movement through plants under differing conditions.
- Identify and explain the role of structures in drawings of plant stems, roots and leaves.
- Make synoptic links with other related topics in this and other modules.

Synoptic links

Questions on transpiration might contain sections on other related topics, such as:
- osmosis — you may be given the water potentials of some cells and asked to predict the movement of water between them
- diffusion and the factors that affect diffusion
- Fick's law and how it predicts the effect of factors on diffusion
- the conflict between regulating water loss and gas exchange (see next section)

The conflict between gas exchange and regulating water loss

Gas exchange surfaces

Key concepts you must understand

Gas exchange surfaces must allow rapid diffusion of respiratory gases across the exchange surface. To do this, they all have a large surface area (relative to the volume to be supplied with the gas), are thin (short diffusion pathway) and maintain a significant difference in concentrations of the gases across the surface.

Fick's law is relevant here:

$$\text{diffusion rate} \propto \frac{\text{surface area of exchange surface} \times \text{concentration difference}}{\text{thickness of exchange surface}}$$

Remember also, from Unit 1: surface area limits the supply rate of oxygen; the volume creates the demand.

The body surface of a protoctistan

Unicellular protoctists, such as *Amoeba*, exchange gases through the plasma membrane of their single cell, which is also their body surface. The large surface area-to-volume ratio means that demand for oxygen is unlikely to outstrip supply.

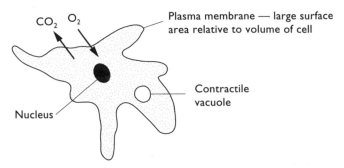

The gill lamellae in the gill filaments of a fish

Fish draw water into the mouth cavity by creating a negative pressure. They lower the floor of the mouth and water enters the mouth cavity. It is then forced over the gills by closing the mouth and raising the floor of the mouth cavity.

As the water passes the gill lamellae, oxygen diffuses from the water into the bloodstream and carbon dioxide diffuses in the opposite direction.

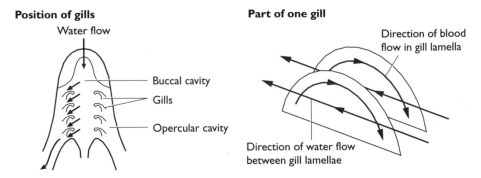

Notice that in the individual lamellae, the blood flows in the opposite direction to the water. This **countercurrent** maintains a concentration gradient for both carbon dioxide and oxygen between the water and the blood and improves the efficiency of gas exchange. An effective surface area-to-volume ratio is provided by the many small gill lamellae.

The tracheoles of an insect

Some water sits in bottom of tube

Lead into tissue

Chitin Rings in walls

Walls are impermiable to gas

The tracheal system of an insect consists of two main **tracheae** that run the length of the insect's body. Smaller tubes, **tracheoles**, branch off the tracheae and carry air directly to the cells of the insect's body. Blood is not involved in the transport of respiratory gases in insects. The tracheae receive air from openings in the insect's body wall called **spiracles**. The large numbers of tracheoles create a large gas exchange surface.

The spongy mesophyll of a leaf

The surface area of the spongy mesophyll cells in contact with the air spaces is large enough to allow effective diffusion of gases.

The principal features of these four exchange surfaces are compared in the table below with the alveoli in mammalian lungs. Although not specified directly in the content for this module, you may be asked to compare different gas exchange surfaces as part of the synoptic assessment.

	Surface of protoctistan	Fish gill lamellae	Insect tracheoles	Spongy mesophyll	Alveoli
Respiratory medium	Water	Water	Air	Air	Air
Exchange surface	Plasma membrane	Lamellae	Tracheoles	Plasma membranes of spongy cells	Alveolar epithelium
Ventilation	None	Movements of mouth create one-way water current	In large insects, abdomen dilates to decrease pressure and draw air in	None	Movements of diaphragm and ribs create two-way air current
Cause of large surface area-to-volume ratio	Small volume of individual cell	Large area of lamellae	Large area of tracheoles	Large area of cell surfaces	Large area of alveoli
How concentration gradient is maintained	Use of oxygen in cell	Countercurrent system in lamellae	Use of oxygen in cells of body	Use of carbon dioxide by mesophyll cells	Ventilation and circulation (see Unit 1)
Thin exchange surface/short diffusion pathway	Plasma membrane is thin	Only a single layer of cells between blood and water	Thin wall of tracheoles	Only cell wall and plasma membrane separate cells and air spaces	Extremely thin epithelium — capillaries close to alveoli

Limiting water loss

Key concepts you must understand

Plants

Water enters the roots and is lost mainly through stomata in the leaf epidermis by transpiration. Carbon dioxide for photosynthesis enters through the stomata.

Excessive water loss would lead to desiccation. To prevent this, the stomata close, but closure restricts the entry of carbon dioxide and so limits photosynthesis. There is a potential conflict between optimising transpiration and photosynthesis.

The extent of the opening is a 'compromise' between the need to allow CO_2 to enter and the need to prevent excessive water loss.

Insects

The tracheal system creates the same problems for an insect. Open spiracles allow exchange of oxygen and carbon dioxide, but also allow water vapour to leave. Circular muscles can contract to close the spiracles (just as stomata can be closed) — but then gas exchange is prevented. The accumulation of carbon dioxide in the tracheae eventually initiates a reaction that opens the spiracles again — but this allows potential dehydration.

Some insects overcome this by 'fluttering' the spiracles. This rapid opening and closing of the spiracles seems to allow effective gas exchange whilst keeping water loss within acceptable limits.

What the examiners will expect you to be able to do

- Explain any of the key concepts.
- Describe the features of a gas exchange surface that allow efficient gas exchange.
- Use Fick's law to explain why the features of a gas exchange surface allow efficient diffusion of gases.
- Interpret data relating total stomatal aperture to the rate of gas exchange and water loss.
- Interpret data relating the rate of flow of water over gills to the rate of gas exchange.
- Interpret data relating insect activity to ventilation movements, rate of gas exchange and water loss.

Synoptic links

Questions on gas exchange may contain sections on other related topics such as:

- aerobic and anaerobic respiration — you may have to link the process using oxygen and producing carbon dioxide to the exchange of gases
- the relationship between surface area and volume and the need for a specialised gas exchange system — for instance, you may be asked to explain why *Amoeba* doesn't need a specialised system but an insect does

- the structure of alveolar epithelial cells in relation to their function
- the factors affecting diffusion and osmosis
- the relationship between Fick's law and the efficiency of a gas exchange surface

The transport of respiratory gases in mammals

Key facts you must know

Oxygen and carbon dioxide are known as respiratory gases because oxygen is used by cells for aerobic respiration and carbon dioxide is produced.

Oxygen is transported in the red blood cells combined with the protein haemoglobin. Haemoglobin consists of four globular polypeptide chains (globins), each containing a 'haem unit' which, because of the iron in it, can bind to oxygen.

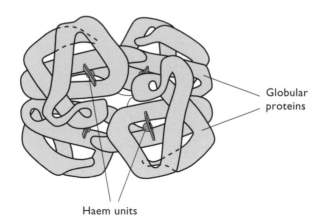

Globular proteins

Haem units

The tertiary structure of haemoglobin allows it to bind effectively with oxygen atoms — each haemoglobin molecule can carry eight oxygen atoms. Haemoglobin can bind (associate) with oxygen atoms where oxygen is plentiful in the surroundings (in the lungs) and release the oxygen (dissociate) when oxygen is scarce (in actively respiring tissues).

Carbon dioxide is transported in a number of ways:
- in physical solution in the plasma (5%)
- combined with the haemoglobin molecule and also with plasma proteins (10%)
- as hydrogencarbonate ions (HCO_3^-) in the plasma (85%)

Haemoglobin and hydrogencarbonate ions act as buffers in the blood plasma. Both can accept hydrogen ions released by acids and so prevent the pH of the blood from falling too low.

Key concepts you must understand

Concentrations of respiratory gases are often expressed as partial pressures in units of kilopascals (kPa). The **partial pressure of oxygen** is often abbreviated to pO_2. Similarly, pCO_2 is an abbreviation for **partial pressure of carbon dioxide**.

The term **oxygen tension** means the same as partial pressure of oxygen.

The percentage of haemoglobin that is associated with oxygen at a given oxygen tension (pO_2) is referred to as the **percentage saturation** of haemoglobin. It varies with the oxygen tension of the surroundings. This is shown in a graph called the **dissociation curve** of haemoglobin.

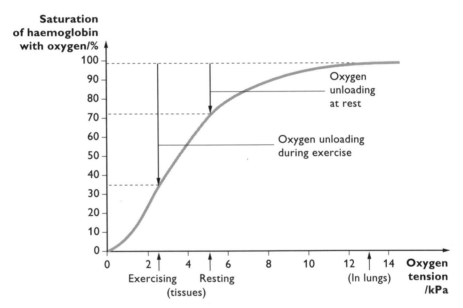

In this example, in the lungs, there is an oxygen tension of 13 kPa and 98% of the haemoglobin is associated with oxygen. In respiring tissues at rest, the oxygen tension is 5.3 kPa and 73% of the haemoglobin is associated with oxygen. 25% of the haemoglobin has unloaded its oxygen (released its oxygen to the tissues). With moderate exercise, the oxygen tension in respiring muscle tissue falls lower — to 2.5 kPa and only 35% of the haemoglobin can remain bound to oxygen. Over 60% of the haemoglobin unloads its oxygen to meet the increased demand.

The association/dissociation of oxygen and haemoglobin is a reversible reaction:

HbO$_2$		Hb	+	O$_2$
oxyhaemoglobin		haemoglobin		oxygen

In any reversible reaction, an equilibrium can be reached. For example, a build-up of oxygen and haemoglobin will limit the dissociation of oxyhaemoglobin and stimulate the association of oxygen with haemoglobin. A reduction in the amount of oxygen or haemoglobin will stimulate more oxyhaemoglobin to dissociate.

In respiring tissue oxyhaemoglobin dissociates and unloads oxygen because:
- oxygen is rapidly used by respiring tissue and so diffuses rapidly from red blood cells, reducing the oxygen tension in the red cells
- the release of carbon dioxide by respiring cells leads to the production of hydrogen ions which bind with free haemoglobin, reducing the concentration of free haemoglobin in the red cells

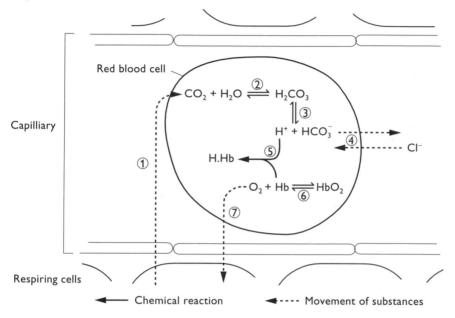

(1) Carbon dioxide from respiration diffuses through the plasma and into the red blood cell.
(2) Carbon dioxide reacts with water to form the weak acid carbonic acid (H_2CO_3). The reaction is catalysed by the enzyme carbonic anhydrase.
(3) Carbonic acid dissociates into hydrogen ions (H^+) and hydrogencarbonate ions (HCO_3^-).
(4) The hydrogencarbonate ions diffuse into the plasma and are replaced by chloride ions (Cl^-) from the plasma. This is known as the **chloride shift**. The chloride shift maintains a low concentration of hydrogencarbonate ions in the red blood cell and stimulates the further dissociation of carbonic acid.
(5) Hydrogen ions bind with free haemoglobin, reducing its concentration in the red blood cell.
(6) More oxyhaemoglobin dissociates into haemoglobin and oxygen.
(7) Oxygen diffuses into respiring cells. This reduces the tension of oxygen in the red blood cell and stimulates further dissociation of oxyhaemoglobin.

Stages (5) and (7) cause a shift in the equilibrium to the right, i.e. they result in increased dissociation of oxyhaemoglobin. The two effects are independent of each other. Any increase in hydrogen ion concentration will stimulate dissociation, *irrespective* of the oxygen tension.

The dissociation of oxygen from haemoglobin is linked to the transport of carbon dioxide as:

- the free haemoglobin can bind with carbon dioxide to form **carbaminohaemoglobin**, which accounts for the transport of 5% of carbon dioxide
- the hydrogencarbonate ions formed from the reactions between water and carbon dioxide in the red blood cell pass into the plasma and account for the transport of 85% of carbon dioxide

During vigorous exercise, muscle cells respire much faster than normal and so produce much more carbon dioxide. This leads to the production of more hydrogen ions, which results in the dissociation of more oxyhaemoglobin. Also, lactate produced by anaerobic respiration leads to still more hydrogen ions being produced. This increase in hydrogen ions (decrease in pH) leads to increased dissociation of oxyhaemoglobin *irrespective* of the oxygen tension, as shown in the graph below.

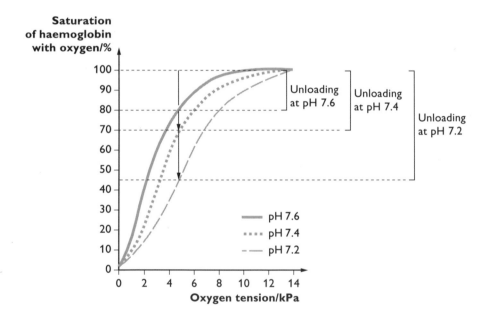

Notice how, as the pH decreases (hydrogen ion concentration increases), the dissociation curve is shifted to the right, resulting in increased unloading of oxygen at any oxygen tension. This is called the **Bohr effect**.

The haemoglobin molecule is similar in all animals that possess it, but there are differences. Some animals live in conditions in which the oxygen tension is much less than the 21 kPa of atmospheric air. These include:

- the llama, which lives at high altitudes (overall air pressure decreases with altitude and so the partial pressure of oxygen must also decrease)
- *Arenicola*, a worm that lives in burrows in sand in the intertidal regions of the sea shore where oxygen tension is low
- the human fetus — the oxygen tension is much lower than in the lungs

In each case, the haemoglobin must have an increased affinity for oxygen. It must be able to remain saturated with oxygen at partial pressures where other haemoglobin molecules would not. The haemoglobin of the human fetus must associate with oxygen at oxygen tensions that cause the maternal oxyhaemoglobin to dissociate.

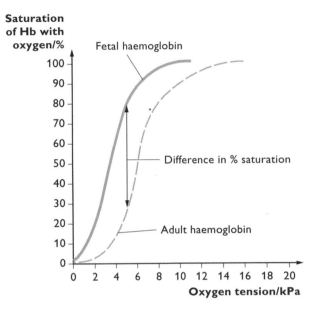

What the examiners will expect you to be able to do

- Recall any of the key facts.
- Explain any of the key concepts.
- Identify different types of haemoglobin from graphs provided.
- Relate the Bohr effect to levels of exercise.
- Explain the different dissociation curves of adult and fetal haemoglobin.

Synoptic links

Questions on transport of respiratory gases may contain sections on other related topics such as:

- the levels of structure of protein molecules, with specific reference to the tertiary and quaternary structures of haemoglobin in relation to its function in oxygen transport
- exercise — how the increased respiration rate in muscles affects dissociation of haemoglobin (you should be able to make relevant comments about the Bohr effect, relating the increased respiration rate to increased levels of carbon dioxide and therefore to increased hydrogen ion concentration)
- the structure of red blood cells related to their function in oxygen transport — you may be asked to relate their structure to efficient gas exchange using Fick's law as a basis (features like thin membrane, large surface area, thin cell so the diffusion distance is short are all relevant points)

- osmotic effects on red blood cells — if red cells are placed in a solution with a higher water potential, they will absorb water, swell and burst whereas if placed in a solution with a lower water potential, they will lose water and shrink
- fetal circulation — a question on fetal haemoglobin may lead into a question about the fetal circulation in general

Digestion and absorption in mammals

Key facts you must know

Digestion breaks down large, sometimes insoluble, molecules into smaller, soluble molecules. This is necessary so that absorption can take place.

Digestion involves **hydrolysis reactions** and the enzymes that catalyse these reactions are hydrolytic **enzymes**. The main hydrolytic reactions of digestion are as follows:

$$\text{Starch} \xrightarrow{\text{amylase}} \text{Maltose} \xrightarrow{\text{maltase}} \alpha\text{-Glucose}$$

$$\text{Cellulose} \xrightarrow{\text{cellulase}} \text{Cellobiose} \xrightarrow{\text{cellobiase}} \beta\text{-Glucose}$$

(Cellulose digestion occurs in herbivorous mammals only.)

$$\text{Triglycerides} \xrightarrow{\text{lipase}} \text{Fatty acids} + \text{Glycerol}$$
(and other lipids)

$$\text{Proteins} \xrightarrow{\text{pepsin/trypsin}} \text{Polypeptides} \xrightarrow{\text{peptidases}} \text{Dipeptides} \xrightarrow{\text{dipeptidases}} \text{Amino acids}$$

The end products of digestion are absorbed in the ileum by a combination of diffusion, facilitated diffusion and active transport. Endocytosis and exocytosis are also involved.

Key concepts you must understand

The gut wall is a barrier to absorption of food materials. Many of the molecules ingested are too large to enter the bloodstream without being **digested**. Digestion hydrolyses large molecules into smaller ones. The smaller molecules can then be **absorbed** and either **respired** or **assimilated**. Molecules that cannot be absorbed are **egested** in the faeces.

Digestion of food

Digestion proceeds by hydrolysis — a process in which bonds are broken by the addition of water molecules. Enzymes catalyse the hydrolysis reactions and ensure that digestion proceeds efficiently.

Digestion of starch

Stage in digestion	Enzymes involved	Notes on reaction
Starch to maltose	Amylase from salivary glands and pancreas	Amylase catalyses the hydrolysis of $\alpha(1,4)$ glycosidic bonds between α-glucose units in the starch molecule Optimum pH is neutral to slightly alkaline Reaction begins in the buccal cavity and recommences in the duodenum Acid pH of the stomach denatures salivary amylase
Maltose to glucose	Maltase in the plasma membranes of the cells of the ileum	Enzymes bound to the plasma membrane of the microvilli hydrolyse $\alpha(1,4)$ glycosidic bonds between the two α-glucose units in maltose molecules

Digestion of triglycerides

Stage in digestion	Enzymes involved	Notes on reaction
Emulsification	None	On leaving the stomach, fats and oils form large droplets with a relatively small surface area-to-volume ratio Bile salts emulsify these droplets — they are chemically unchanged, but form much smaller droplets with a much larger collective surface area, making subsequent enzyme action more efficient Bile salts form a hydrophilic shell around each droplet, making it water soluble
Hydrolysis to fatty acids and glycerol	Lipase from pancreas	In the duodenum and ileum, lipase hydrolyses the ester bonds between glycerol and fatty acid units in triglyceride molecules The fatty acids and glycerol, coated with bile salts, form a micelle Sodium hydrogencarbonate from the pancreas provides the optimum, slightly alkaline, pH for the enzyme

Digestion of protein

Stage in digestion	Enzymes involved	Notes on reaction
Protein to short-chain polypeptides	Pepsin in stomach and trypsin from pancreas	Both enzymes are endopeptidases — they hydrolyse peptide bonds in the middle of protein molecules, making more 'ends' available for exopeptidases to act on Both enzymes are secreted in inactive form (pepsinogen and trypsinogen) to prevent digestion of the cells that produce them Pepsinogen is activated by hydrochloric acid in the stomach and trypsinogen by enterokinase, an enzyme from the wall of the small intestine
Short-chain polypeptides to dipeptides	Exopeptidases from the pancreas (carboxypeptidases and aminopeptidases)	These enzymes hydrolyse peptide bonds at the ends of polypeptide chains Carboxypeptidases attack the carboxyl end of the molecules Aminopeptidases attack the amino end of the molecule
Dipeptides to amino acids	Dipeptidases in the plasma membranes of epithelial cells in the small intestine	Dipeptidases hydrolyse the peptide bonds in the dipeptides, releasing free amino acids

[handwritten annotations: "HCl", "entero peptidase"]

The next table gives a summary of all the processes involved in digestion in a typical mammal.

Region of gut	Secretion	Enzymes	Substrates acted on	Product(s) of digestion
Buccal cavity (mouth)	Saliva (from salivary glands)	Amylase	Starch	Maltose
Stomach	Gastric juice	Pepsin	Proteins	Short-chain polypeptides
Lumen of duodenum and ileum	Pancreatic juice (from pancreas)	Amylase Lipase Trypsin Exopeptidases	Starch Triglycerides Protein Short-chain polypeptides	Maltose Glycerol and fatty acids Short chain polypeptides Dipeptides
Wall of ileum		Maltase Dipeptidase	Maltose Dipeptides	α-Glucose Amino acids

Herbivorous mammals also digest cellulose. They do not produce their own cellulase, but rely on microorganisms living in some region of their gut in a **mutualistic** association. In the case of ruminant herbivores (such as cattle and sheep), there are billions of microorganisms in the rumen — a large pouch associated with the stomach of the animal.

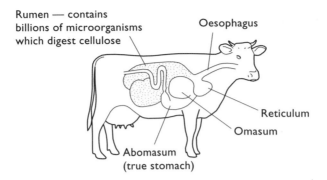

When ruminants swallow their food it passes into the rumen. Here, microorganisms (mainly bacteria and unicellular protoctistans) digest the cellulose and ferment the β-glucose produced. The products of this fermentation include methane and short-chain fatty acids. The fatty acids are absorbed through the stomach wall into the blood stream. The methane is belched out, adding to the greenhouse gases.

Ruminant herbivores feed largely on grasses but can produce substantial amounts of body tissue, mainly muscle, from this protein-poor diet. This is possible because:
- most of the protein in the grass is digested by the cow to amino acids
- the non-protein nitrogenous compounds in the grass (such as DNA, RNA and ATP) are used by the microorganisms in the rumen to make microbial protein
- when the microorganisms die, they pass into the abomasum where their protein is digested along with the grass protein — the cattle get an extra supply of protein

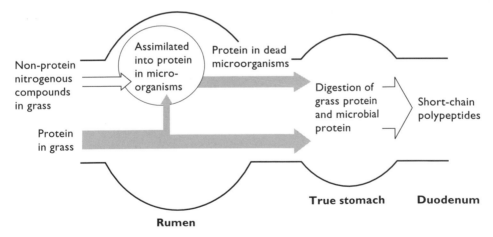

Secretion of digesive juices in mammals is controlled by both nerves and hormones (see page 52).

Absorption of the products of digestion

A little absorption takes place in the stomach (about 20% of alcohol is absorbed there). However, most takes place in the small intestine, particularly in the ileum.

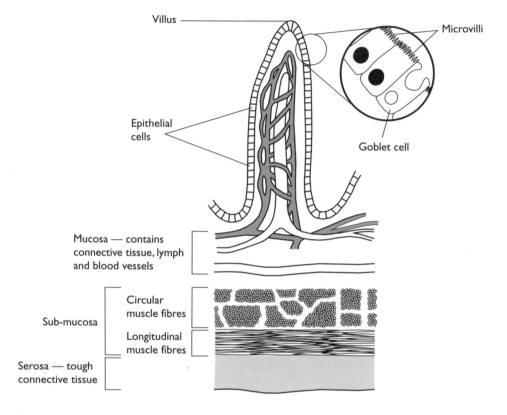

Tip Make sure that you distinguish carefully in the examination between villi and microvilli — they are not the same structures and you will lose marks if you confuse them.

The ileum is adapted to its function in the following ways:

- it has a large absorbing surface area because
  - it is long (about 3.5 metres)
  - the internal wall has circular folds
  - the folds are covered in villi
  - most epithelial cells of the villi have microvilli (about 1500 per cell)
- the epithelial cells are thin, giving a short diffusion distance and allowing easy uptake of the products of digestion
- it has a good blood supply (at rest, between 20% and 25% of the cardiac output)
- the circular and longitudinal muscle fibres in the wall allow
  - peristalsis (a wave-like progressive contraction and relaxation of the muscles which moves food along the intestines)

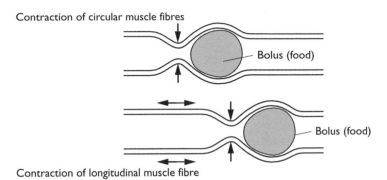

— segmentation, in which portions of the intestine can be separated from the next by contraction of the circular muscle fibres

Mechanisms of absorption

Sodium ions

Some sodium ions pass into the epithelial cells by diffusion through ion channel proteins in the plasma membrane. They are then actively transported from the epithelial cells into the bloodstream. The active transport into the blood maintains a low concentration of sodium ions in the epithelial cells, allowing continuous uptake.

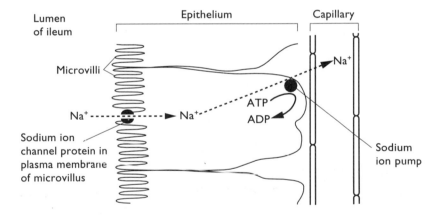

Glucose

Most glucose absorption is coupled with the absorption of sodium ions. It is actively transported from the epithelial cells into the blood to maintain a low glucose concentration in the cells. Glucose then enters passively from the lumen of the ileum, mainly by a sodium ion/glucose co-transport protein. Because the two are linked, glucose absorption is reduced if the sodium ion gradient is not maintained.

Amino acids

Amino acids are absorbed in the same way. Active transport into the blood drives uptake from the ileum by a sodium ion/amino acid co-transport protein.

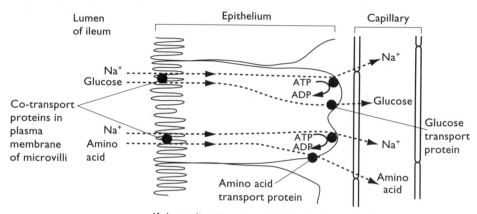

If the sodium ion concentration in the epithelial cell becomes too high, the co-transport proteins will not take up as much glucose/amino acid

Fatty acids and glycerol

Both are lipid-soluble and so can diffuse from the lumen of the ileum through the plasma membranes into the epithelial cells. No transport protein is needed. Once inside the cells, some fatty acids and glycerol diffuse into the bloodstream. Most, however, are recombined into triglyceride molecules. These are combined with protein molecules by the Golgi bodies and 'packaged' into **chylomicrons**. The water-soluble chylomicrons leave the epithelial cells by exocytosis and enter the lacteals (lymph vessels) in the villi. The chylomicrons enter the blood when the lymph empties into the subclavian veins (veins from the arms).

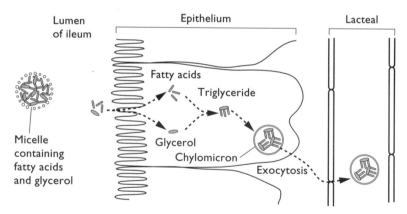

What the examiners will expect you to be able to do

- Recall any of the key facts.
- Explain any of the key concepts.
- Identify specific enzymes from information giving substrates and/or products.
- Identify type of peptidase (exo- or endopeptidase) from information giving site of hydrolysis of protein chain.

- Identify mechanisms of absorption (diffusion, active transport etc.) from diagrams/other information.

Synoptic links

Questions on digestion may contain sections on other related topics such as:
- the structure of biological molecules, e.g. carbohydrates, triglycerides and proteins — you may be required to complete diagrams showing the structure of these molecules or relate the structure to solubility or ease of transport across a membrane
- condensation and hydrolysis — you may be asked to complete diagrams showing these processes or to identify the processes from diagrams
- enzyme action — you may be asked to relate the changing conditions of pH in the gut to the optimum activity of the various enzymes secreted
- the structure of plasma membranes, with particular reference to different methods of transport across them
- food tests — you may be asked to describe a test to identify reducing sugar, non-reducing sugar, lipid or protein
- the structure of cells — you may be asked to identify cell organelles in a drawing or photograph of an epithelial cell
- microscopy and magnification — you may be asked to calculate the magnification of a photograph or to use features in the photograph to identify the type of microscope (electron or light) used

Diet, digestion and life histories

Key concepts you must understand

We do not eat the same diet throughout our lives. For several months, we are fed solely on milk. For this period, the enzyme rennin is produced in our stomachs specifically to curdle the milk protein and make it more digestible. When milk ceases to be the only, or main, source of food, rennin is no longer produced.

There are other examples of enzyme production changing to adapt to changes in diet at different stages of a life history. Some animals have two distinct phases in their life history:
- a larval phase in which the animal grows but does not reproduce
- an adult reproductive phase

The change in body form that often takes place is called **metamorphosis**. In some animals (e.g. frogs), the change occurs gradually. Over a period of several weeks, the tadpole grows larger, the tail is reabsorbed and the gills are lost. In other cases, the animal enters a pupal stage in which a total reorganisation of the body tissues takes place in a relatively short period of time. Examples of such a life history include those of many insects, such as the *Lepidoptera* — butterflies and moths.

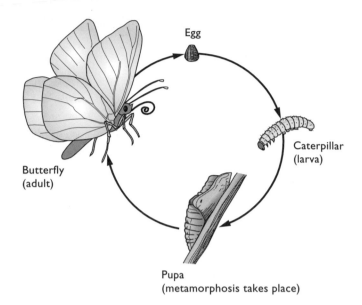

Egg

Caterpillar
(larva)

Butterfly
(adult)

Pupa
(metamorphosis takes place)

Both the mouthparts and enzymes in the two stages show adaptations to the diet. The larva has mandibles to cut and grind the leaves on which it feeds. The adult has a proboscis with which to suck nectar from flowers. The digestive enzymes produced in the two stages are related to the diet as shown in the following table.

Stage of life cycle	Food	Enzymes produced	
		Salivary glands	Mid gut
Caterpillar (larva)	Foliage (leaves)	–	Amylase, maltase, sucrase, exopeptidases, endopeptidases, dipeptidases, lipase (very small amounts)
Butterfly (adult)	Nectar	Sucrase	–

The enzymes produced by the larva enable the digestion of the starch and protein found in foliage to glucose and amino acids respectively, which can then be absorbed and used. There is very little lipid in foliage.

Only sucrase is produced by the adult. This hydrolyses sucrose in nectar to glucose and fructose. These monosaccharides can be respired to release energy. As no other nutrients are obtained, the adult cannot live long and must find a mate quickly.

What the examiners will expect you to be able to do

You must be able to recall this specific example, but you must also be able to apply the concept of growth and reproductive stages to the life cycles of other animals. You may be required to interpret data on the life cycles of other types of insect or animals from other Phyla.

Receptors in animals

Receptors are **energy transducers**; they convert some kind of energy into a **generator potential**, which may then initiate an **action potential** in a nerve cell. An action potential passing along a nerve cell is a **nerve impulse**.

There are many different receptors, but the only ones you are required to know about are **Pacinian corpuscles** and the **rod** and **cone cells** in the retina of the eye.

The Pacinian corpuscle and pressure detection

Key facts you must know

Pacinian corpuscles are pressure sensors found mainly deep in the dermis of the skin. They are also found in some joints and tendons.

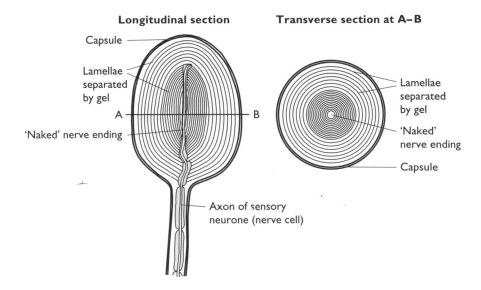

Key concepts you must understand

Pressure on the skin is transmitted to the corpuscle. If the pressure is great enough it deforms the corpuscle sufficiently to excite pressure-sensitive ion channels in the membrane of the naked nerve ending. These open and positively charged sodium ions move inwards and alter the balance of charge across the membrane (the **membrane potential**). This change in membrane potential is called the **generator potential**. A greater pressure deforms the Pacinian corpuscle more and opens more ion channels. This produces a larger generator potential.

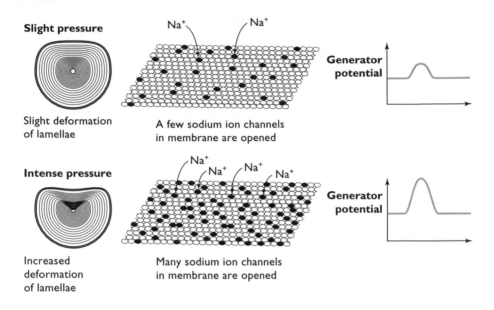

Slight pressure

Slight deformation of lamellae

A few sodium ion channels in membrane are opened

Generator potential

Intense pressure

Increased deformation of lamellae

Many sodium ion channels in membrane are opened

Generator potential

If the generator potential is large enough, a nerve impulse will be initiated.

The eye and light detection

Key facts you must know

You must be able to identify key structures in the eye and know their function.

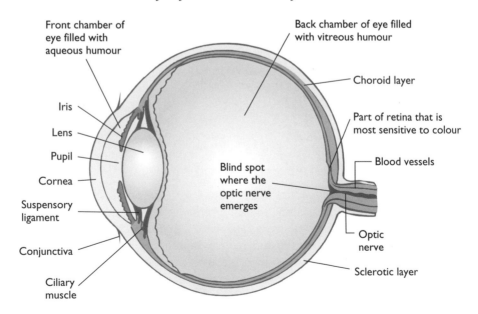

Front chamber of eye filled with aqueous humour

Back chamber of eye filled with vitreous humour

Choroid layer

Iris

Lens

Pupil

Cornea

Suspensory ligament

Conjunctiva

Ciliary muscle

Part of retina that is most sensitive to colour

Blood vessels

Blind spot where the optic nerve emerges

Optic nerve

Sclerotic layer

Part of eye	Description	Function in focusing and detection of light
Conjunctiva	Very thin, transparent membrane covering the cornea and lining the eyelids	Transmission of light due to transparency
Cornea	Transparent front part of the wall of the eye	Transmission of light due to transparency; refraction of light due to curvature
Aqueous and vitreous humours	Fluids in the eye; aqueous humour is less viscous than vitreous humour	Transmission of light due to transparency
Iris	Coloured disc in front of the lens	Controls the amount of light entering the eye
Lens	Transparent crystalline structure held in place by suspensory ligaments	Transmission of light due to transparency; refraction of light due to curvature
Ciliary muscles	Ring of muscle outside lens	Controls convexity of lens and therefore its ability to refract light; muscles contract to produce a more convex powerful lens; relaxation produces a less convex, less powerful lens
Retina	Inner layer of wall of eye containing rods and cones	Rods and cones transduce light energy into generator potentials; fovea has the greatest concentration of cones; blind spot has no sense cells
Choroid	Black middle layer of wall of eye	Dark colour prevents internal reflection of light rays

Key concepts you must understand

The eye is able to focus all rays of light from one point on an object to a single point on the retina.

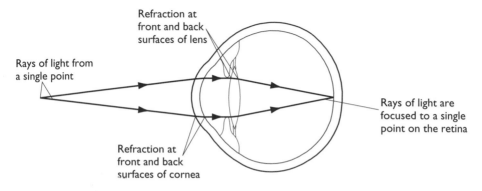

The ability of the eye to adjust focusing from near to distant objects is called **accommodation**.

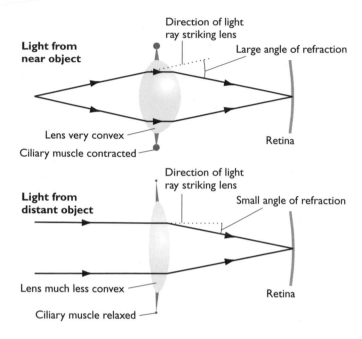

The amount of refraction taking place at the cornea is more or less constant, as the curvature remains the same. The curvature of the lens is altered by the action of the ciliary muscles and so the amount of refraction changes.

Cones and rods in the retina are linked to nerve cells by **bipolar cells**. Cones and rods differ in **visual acuity** (the degree of detail in which the object is perceived) and in **sensitivity** (the intensity of light required to produce a sufficiently large generator potential to initiate an action potential) because of the way in which they are connected to the bipolar cells.

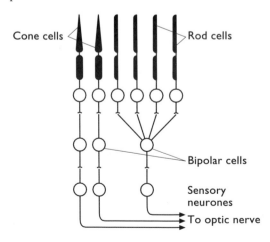

Tip In an examination diagram, the connections to bipolar cells may not be shown; the rods and cones may be shown connected directly to nerve cells.

Property	Cones	Rods
Sensitivity	Low: light energy transduced by a single cone must produce a generator potential large enough to exceed the threshold needed for an action potential. In low light intensities this is unlikely	High: in low light intensities, generator potentials from several rods can combine and so the threshold is more likely to be exceeded and an action potential initiated. This phenomenon is called summation. It is possible because several rods are linked to (or converge on) one neurone (via bipolar cells). This is called retinal convergence
Acuity	High: each cone is connected to a single bipolar cell, so in high light intensities each cone stimulated represents a separate part of the image which can be seen in detail	Low: several rods are connected to the same bipolar cell, so the individual parts of the image represented by each rod are merged into one — they are indistinguishable and detail is poor

Rods and cones are distributed unevenly across the retina.

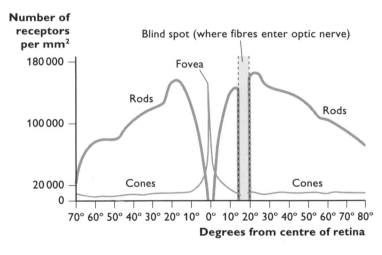

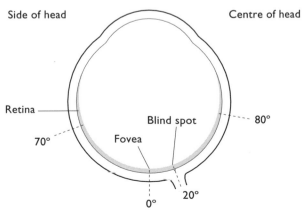

The greatest concentration of cones is found at the fovea in the centre of the retina. Looking straight at an object focuses light from it onto the fovea, enabling it to be seen in great detail if the light intensity is high. The greatest concentration of rods is about 20° away from the fovea. In very low light intensities, looking slightly to the side of an object causes the light rays to fall on this area of the retina. Summation by the rods allows better perception than if light fell on the fovea.

There are three different types of cone, sensitive to different wavelengths of light which are broadly equivalent to the three primary colours — red, blue and green.

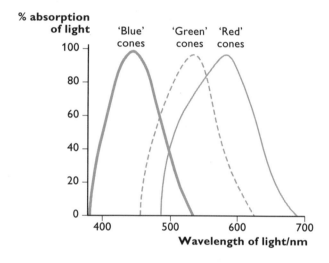

A wavelength of 550 nm stimulates both red and green cones and is interpreted by the brain as yellow.

When sense cells in the eye are stimulated by light, a change occurs in a photo-sensitive pigment. This alters the membrane potential of the cell, creating a generator potential. The pigment in rods is **rhodopsin** and the changes that occur on stimulation are shown in the diagram.

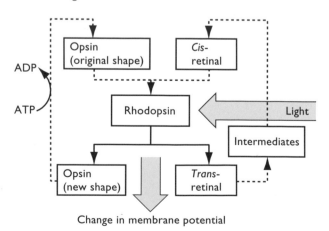

Change in membrane potential

What the examiners will expect you to be able to do

- Recall any of the key facts.
- Explain any of the key concepts.
- Interpret data relating intensity of stimulus to the amplitude of generator potential and frequency of action potentials.
- Interpret diagrams of connections of rods and cones to bipolar cells/nerve cells to explain acuity and sensitivity.
- Interpret graphs showing the extent of stimulation of the three types of cone by different wavelengths of light.
- Relate the position of image formation on the retina to the ability to perceive colour and/or detail.
- Relate the intensity of pressure stimulation to the frequency of action potentials.

Synoptic links

Questions on receptors may contain sections on other related topics such as:

- respiration — the changes produced in receptors by energy transduction must be restored using energy from respiration; you may be asked to account for the presence of mitochondria in sense cells
- transport across membranes — changes in membrane potential involve movement of ions passively and by active transport; you may have to identify the type of transport occurring or describe differences between some of the processes

Transmission of information through the nervous system

Action potentials transmit information along nerve cells (neurones)

change in mem potential.

Key facts you must know

A nerve impulse results from an action potential (change in the membrane potential) being initiated at one end of the neurone and being propagated along the neurone. Information is therefore transmitted as a series of action potentials.

Tip Remember, a nerve impulse is not like an electric current; nothing actually moves along the neurone. Think of a Mexican wave in a sports stadium — nobody leaves their seat or moves around the stadium, yet the wave is passed along.

There are many types of neurone, but two are of special importance:

- **sensory neurones**, which carry nerve impulses from receptors into the central nervous system
- **motor neurones** (shown below), which carry nerve impulses from the central nervous system to effectors (muscles and glands)

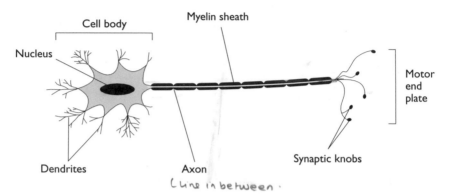

L une in between.

Key concepts you must understand

Action potentials can be initiated and transmitted along neurones because of the specialised plasma membrane of the axons of these cells. It can maintain an electrical potential difference between the inside and outside of the membrane. This is called the **resting potential** and typically, at rest, the inside of the axon is about 70 mV (millivolts) more negative than the outside. $= \uparrow K^+ inside.$

The resting potential is maintained by:
1. • large anions, for example negatively charged proteins inside the axon
2. • passive diffusion of sodium and potassium ions across the membrane
3. • active transport of sodium and potassium ions across the membrane

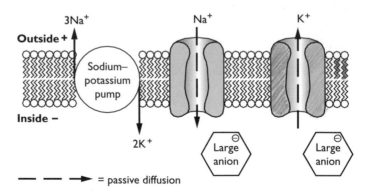

The imbalance of the transport systems, coupled with the charge on the large anions (proteins), leaves the inside of the membrane with a resting potential of –70 mV (with respect to the outside). The membrane is **polarised**.

If the membrane of a neurone is stimulated, then an action potential may result. Some 'gated' ion channels in the membrane open and allow positively charged sodium ions to enter. This reduces the resting potential. If it is reduced to –55 mV, an action potential will result because, at this potential difference, thousands more 'voltage-activated' sodium ion channels open, allowing sodium ions to 'flood' in. These positive ions quickly reduce the resting potential and even allow the inside of the membrane to become positively charged with respect to the outside. The membrane has been **depolarised**.

If the critical potential of –55 mV is not reached, these voltage activated gates will not open, sodium ions cannot flood in and no action potential can be produced.

So, the size of the action potential does not vary: there either *is* an action potential or there *isn't*. It is an **all-or-nothing response**. The critical value of ~~–55 mV~~ is known as the **threshold value**. ↳ All or nothing

Once an action potential has been generated, it is propagated along the axon because it stimulates depolarisation in successive regions of the axon membrane.

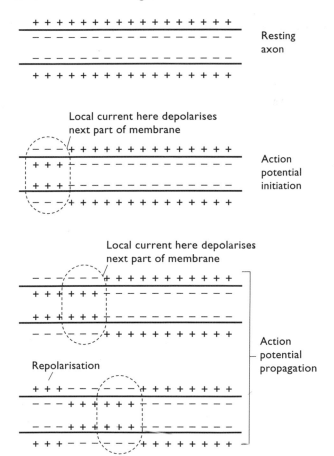

In the region of the original action potential, the membrane must **repolarise** (be restored to the resting potential) before another action potential can be generated. Repolarisation occurs when, at the height of the influx of the sodium ions, potassium ion gates open and positively charged potassium ions flood out. This makes the inside of the membrane once again 70 mV negative with respect to the outside, and another action potential can be generated.

The events of depolarisation and repolarisation can be shown on a graph of membrane potential against time.

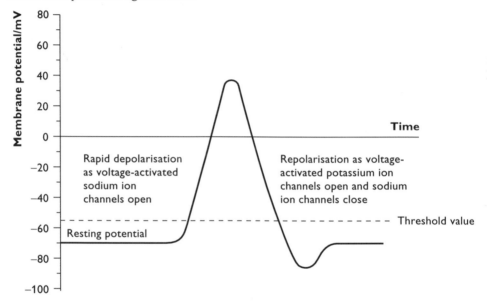

The period of time when an action potential cannot be generated is called the **refractory period**. This limits the transmission of nerve impulses (action potentials):

- an action potential can only be transmitted away from the area in which it was generated — not back towards it (the area 'behind' the action potential is repolarising)
- there is an upper limit to the frequency of transmission of action potentials due to the time taken to repolarise (most neurones can still manage several hundred per second)

The speed of transmission of an action potential is affected by several factors. These include:

- temperature — like all physiological processes, an increase in temperature will increase the rate of the process, up to the point where enzymes and transport proteins begin to denature
- diameter of the neurone — neurones with a large diameter conduct impulses faster than those with a narrow diameter
- myelination — myelinated neurones conduct impulses faster than non-myelinated neurones

Myelinated neurones are capable of **saltatory conduction**. In a non-myelinated neurone, each portion of the axon depolarises in turn and the action potential is propagated along the entire axon. In myelinated neurones, the action potential is only generated at the nodes of Ranvier — the 'gaps' in the myelination. The nerve impulse 'jumps' from node to node and so is conducted much faster than in non-myelinated neurones.

Chemicals transmit information between nerve cells (neurones) at synapses

Key facts you must know

At a synapse, only a minute distance separates the membranes of two neurones. Chemical transmitters (**neurotransmitters**) are released from the membrane of the **pre-synaptic neurone**, cross the **synaptic cleft** and bind to receptors on the membrane of the **post-synaptic neurone**.

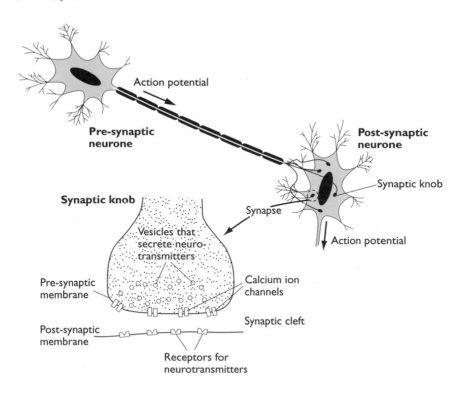

When an action potential arrives at the pre-synaptic membrane, it causes the vesicles to release a transmitter substance (neurotransmitter) into the synaptic cleft. This binds to receptor proteins in the post-synaptic membrane.

Key concepts you must understand

Synapses can be excitatory or inhibitory; that is, they can promote the initiation of an action potential in the post-synaptic neurone or they can inhibit it (make it less likely to occur).

The essence of transmission is the same at excitatory and inhibitory synapses. However, the neurotransmitter is different and so is the effect on the post-synaptic membrane. The events are summarised in the following flow chart.

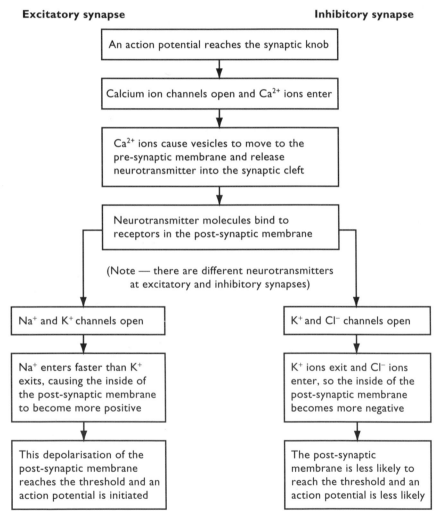

Excitatory synapse   **Inhibitory synapse**

An action potential reaches the synaptic knob

Calcium ion channels open and Ca^{2+} ions enter

Ca^{2+} ions cause vesicles to move to the pre-synaptic membrane and release neurotransmitter into the synaptic cleft

Neurotransmitter molecules bind to receptors in the post-synaptic membrane

(Note — there are different neurotransmitters at excitatory and inhibitory synapses)

Na^+ and K^+ channels open	K^+ and Cl^- channels open
Na^+ enters faster than K^+ exits, causing the inside of the post-synaptic membrane to become more positive	K^+ ions exit and Cl^- ions enter, so the inside of the post-synaptic membrane becomes more negative
This depolarisation of the post-synaptic membrane reaches the threshold and an action potential is initiated	The post-synaptic membrane is less likely to reach the threshold and an action potential is less likely

Often, when a neurotransmitter has bound to its receptor and produced the effect, it is hydrolysed and the component parts released back into the synaptic cleft. These diffuse back into the pre-synaptic cell and are absorbed and reassembled into the neurotransmitter, using energy from ATP produced in respiration. There are usually many mitochondria in this region of a neurone to supply the ATP.

Usually, many neurones, not just two, synapse together. Some of the synapses might be excitatory, others might be inhibitory and their effects on the post-synaptic cell are the result of the **summation** of all their individual effects.

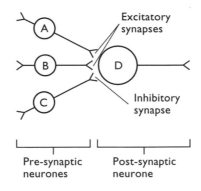

| | Pre-synaptic neurones | Post-synaptic neurone |

Action potential in presynaptic neurones	Action potential in neurone D	Reasons
A	✗	Sub-threshold stimulation — voltage-activated sodium channels are not opened
B	✗	Sub-threshold stimulation — voltage-activated sodium channels are not opened
A + B	✓	The summation of effects of neurotransmitter of both excitatory synapses exceeds the threshold
A + C	✗	The summation of effects of excitatory and inhibitory synapses results in little change in the membrane potential — the threshold is not reached

Detecting the intensity of a stimulus

The links between stimulus transduction and generation of an action potential vary between different receptors but, in general, the following hold true:

- an increase in intensity of the stimulus results in a *larger* generator potential in the receptor cell (an increase in *amplitude* of the generator potential)
- an increased generator potential results in *more* action potentials (an increase in *frequency* of the action potentials)

What the examiners will expect you to be able to do

- Recall any of the key facts.
- Explain any of the key concepts.
- Interpret diagrams showing changes in membrane potential.
- Interpret diagrams of nerve networks showing summation at synapses.
- Interpret diagrams of synapses.
- Explain the specificity of receptor proteins in the post-synaptic membrane.

- Relate stimulus intensity to the size of generator potentials and the *frequency* of action potentials.

> **Synoptic links**
>
> Questions on nerve impulses may contain sections on other related topics such as:
> - cell structure — you may be asked to relate the presence of specific organelles in neurones (e.g. mitochondria) to their function
> - biological molecules — you may be asked to relate protein structure to the specificity of post-synaptic receptors
> - transport across membranes — changes in membrane potential involve the movement of ions both passively and by active transport; you may have to identify the type of transport occurring or describe differences between some of the processes

Integration and control by nerves and hormones

Nervous control

Key facts you must know

Our nervous system is divided physically into two major components:
- the **central nervous system** (CNS), comprising the brain and spinal cord
- the **peripheral nervous system**, comprising the cranial and spinal nerves, each containing many hundreds of sensory and motor neurones

Our nervous system is divided functionally into:
- the **somatic nervous system** (SNS), which integrates information from the special senses to produce responses in skeletal muscles
- the **autonomic nervous system** (ANS), which integrates information from receptors in internal organs and produces responses in the same or other organs or glands

The ANS is subdivided into:
- the visceral sensory branch, which transmits sensory nerve impulses into the central nervous system
- the sympathetic branch, which transmits impulses from the central nervous system to the organs, generally preparing the body for 'fight or flight' — for example by increasing cardiac output and pulmonary ventilation
- the parasympathetic branch, which acts antagonistically to the sympathetic branch and prepares the body for 'rest and repair', decreasing cardiac output and pulmonary ventilation

Both the somatic nervous system and the autonomic nervous system have components in the central nervous system and in the peripheral nervous system, as the following diagram shows.

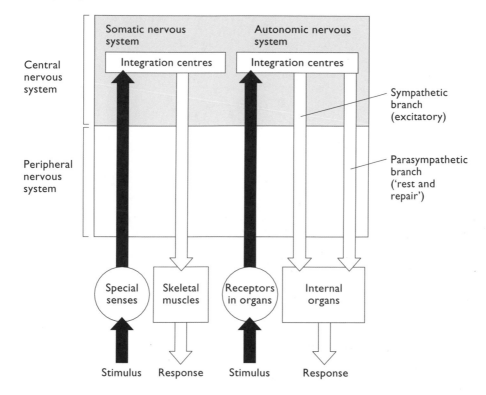

Neurones are sometimes organised into simple **reflex arcs**. In a reflex arc, a few (usually two or three) neurones synapse with each other in sequence so that an impulse passing along the first *must* pass along the others in the arc. The consequence of this is that stimulating the sense cell that initiates the action potential in the first neurone always produces the same response.

The general layout of a three-neurone reflex arc is:

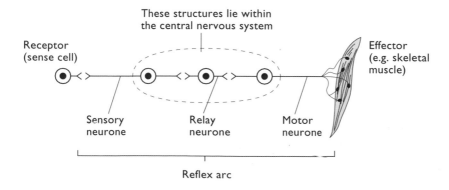

Reflex arcs in which the synapses with the relay neurone occur in the brain control **cranial reflexes**, whilst those in which the synapses occur in the spinal cord control **spinal reflexes**.

Many **somatic** reflexes are protective, such as the withdrawal reflex.

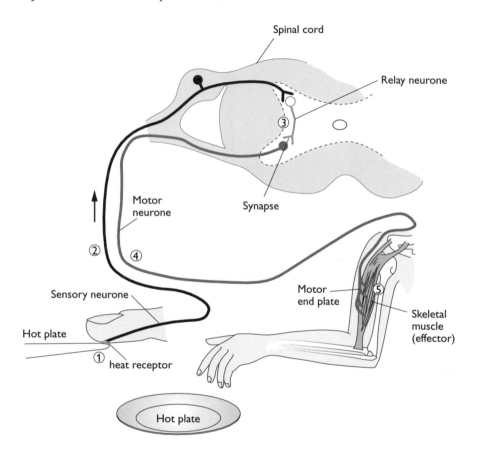

(1) The heat receptor is stimulated by the hot plate and a generator potential results.
(2) The generator potential initiates an action potential in the sensory neurone, which is transmitted along the neurone.
(3) At the synapse with the relay neurone, neurotransmitter is released and initiates an action potential in the relay neurone.
(4) This is repeated at the synapse between the relay neurone and the motor neurone and an action potential is transmitted along the motor neurone.
(5) At the motor end plate, the action potential stimulates the contraction of the skeletal muscle, causing the automatic withdrawal of the hand from the hot plate.

Autonomic reflexes control many of the bodily functions, such as heart rate and breathing rate. The sympathetic and parasympathetic branches act antagonistically.

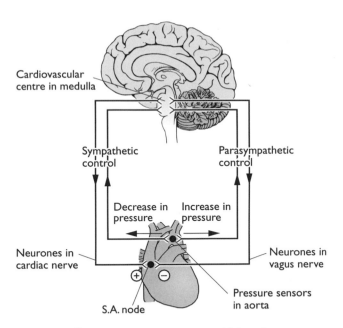

Cardiovascular centre in medulla

Sympathetic control

Parasympathetic control

Decrease in pressure

Increase in pressure

Neurones in cardiac nerve

Neurones in vagus nerve

Pressure sensors in aorta

S.A. node

⊕ Increases rate of discharge of S.A. node
⊖ Decreases rate of discharge of S.A. node

Sympathetic control	Parasympathetic control
Initiated by a decrease in blood pressure in the aorta	Initiated by an increase in blood pressure in the aorta
Impulses pass to the cardiovascular centre and then to the sino-atrial node in the heart via neurones in the cardiac nerve	Impulses pass to the cardiovascular centre and then to the sino-atrial node in the heart via neurones in the vagus nerve
Noradrenaline is released from endings of parasympathetic neurones in the sino-atrial node, which increases activity of the node and so increases heart rate	Acetylcholine is released from endings of parasympathetic neurones in the sino-atrial node, which reduces activity of the node and so reduces heart rate
Other branches of the cardiac nerve affect the ventricle muscle and increase stroke volume	Other branches of the vagus nerve affect the ventricle muscle and reduce stroke volume

Hormonal control

Key facts you must know

Hormones are chemicals produced by **endocrine glands**. They target particular cells in the body because of receptor proteins on or in these cells. The tertiary structure of these proteins has a binding site that is complementary to only one hormone.

Key concepts you must understand

Hormones activate processes in cells in one of two main ways:

- steroid hormones (like the reproductive hormones) are small, lipid-soluble molecules that can pass freely through plasma membranes and bind with receptors on the nuclear envelope; the receptor/hormone complex is then able to activate specific genes
- non-steroid hormones (such as insulin) bind to receptors on the surface of the cell, which stimulates the production of cyclic AMP in the cell; the cAMP acts as a 'second messenger', activating enzymes which produce specific metabolic effects (see pages 57–58 for the action of insulin)

The action of hormones is different from that of nerves in several ways. Hormone controlled responses are:

- slower, because the hormone is secreted into, and travels in, the bloodstream to reach its target cells
- longer lasting, because the effect persists for as long as the hormone remains bound to its receptor in or on the target cell
- more general in their effects, because hormones often have target cells in different regions of the body — some hormones affect nearly all cells

The control of digestive secretions is controlled by nerves *and* hormones.

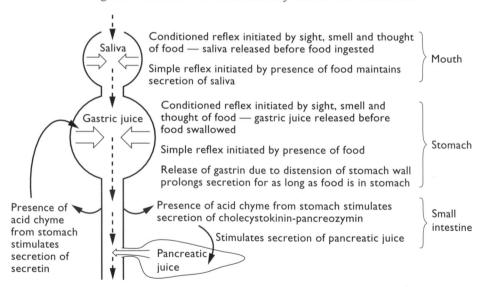

This illustrates some of the differences between nervous and hormonal control:

- simple and conditioned reflexes initiate the secretion of both saliva and gastric juice; these are quick, short-lasting effects which prepare the organs and ensure that some digestive enzymes are present as soon as food enters
- hormone-controlled responses maintain the level of secretions for as long as the food is present; these longer-lasting responses are essential to ensure complete digestion of the food

What the examiners will expect you to be able to do

- Recall any of the key facts.
- Explain any of the key concepts.
- Interpret information about responses and deduce whether they are controlled by hormones or by nerves.
- Compare and contrast nervous and hormonal control.
- Interpret diagrams concerning the mode of action of hormones.

Animal behaviour

Key facts you must know

- Much of the behaviour of invertebrates can be classified into two types: **taxes** (singular, **taxis**) and **kineses** (singular, **kinesis**). Both of these are non-intelligent behaviour.
- Taxes are characterised by movement either towards or away from a **directional** stimulus. Maggots move away from light; many insects are attracted by and move towards pheromones (chemicals similar to hormones).
- Kineses are characterised by increased or decreased movement as the **intensity** of a stimulus changes. Woodlice move around more in dry conditions and less in moist conditions.

Key concepts you must understand

- Both taxes and kineses have survival value.
- A maggot, once fully fed and fully grown, pupates (metamorphoses) in a dark place, where it is less likely to be preyed upon, so the **negative phototaxis** (movement away from light) enables it to achieve this.
- Woodlice lose water easily and dehydrate in dry conditions. By moving less in moist conditions, they are likely to *remain* in those conditions. By moving more in dry conditions, they are likely to *leave* the dry conditions and find moist conditions.

Synoptic links

Questions on integration by nerves and hormones may contain sections on other related topics such as:

- transmission of nerve impulses
- regulation of the function of bodily processes — you may be given data concerning a body function and the effects of hormones or nervous stimulation on that process (e.g. heart rate and breathing rate)
- biological molecules — you may be given information concerning the shape of hormone molecules and receptor sites on plasma membranes
- natural selection — you may be asked to relate patterns of behaviour to a survival advantage

Homeostasis

Key facts you must know

Homeostasis literally means 'steady-standing'. Homeostatic mechanisms maintain a constant internal environment.

The cells of the body are bathed in a fluid of near constant temperature, pH, water potential and many other factors. This unchanging environment allows enzymes to function with optimum efficiency, regardless of the external conditions. Homeostasis gives an organism a degree of independence from its surroundings.

The liver is an important homeostatic organ because:
- it is a large active organ which generates large amounts of heat energy; this is important to mammals in maintaining a constantly high internal body temperature
- it is the main site of interconversion of glucose and glycogen controlled by insulin and glucagon; this maintains a stable plasma glucose concentration
- it is the site of deamination of surplus amino acids, resulting in the formation of the excretory product urea

Key concepts you must understand

Mammals are able to maintain constant:
- internal temperature
- plasma glucose concentration
- plasma water potential

These factors are maintained by **negative feedback** systems. In negative feedback, a deviation from a normal 'set' value is detected and brings about a series of changes that restore the set value.

Controlling internal temperature

Mammals are **endotherms** — they maintain a constant internal temperature, despite changing environmental conditions, by using physiological processes and metabolic energy. They can also use behavioural techniques (e.g. seeking shade). Endotherms are sometimes referred to as warm-blooded.

Reptiles are **ectotherms** — they have a limited capacity to regulate internal body temperature, which therefore fluctuates with that of the surroundings. They are sometimes referred to as cold-blooded. However, ectotherms may exert some control over body temperature through behavioural adaptations such as basking in the sun, seeking shade, nocturnal habits.

Tip Size matters! Large reptiles have much more control over their body temperature than small ones. The bulk of a large animal takes longer to warm up and to cool down and so the temperature does not fluctuate so much. It is a question of surface area and volume. As size increases, the volume (which is a measure of how many cells lose or gain heat) increases faster than the surface area — through which heat is lost and gained.

Body temperature will remain constant if heat losses balance heat gains.

Mammals gain heat by:

- radiation from other objects — we can all feel the effects of solar radiation on a hot summer day
- eating warm food — the heat energy in the food is transferred to the body
- respiration — much of the energy released in respiration is transduced to heat; very active organs such as the liver and active skeletal muscle generate large amounts of heat

Mammals lose heat by conduction, convection, radiation and evaporation. The contributions of these methods are summarised in the table below.

Method of heat loss	Description of method	Involvement in temperature regulation in mammals
Conduction	Heat energy is transferred by direct contact — heat energy moves to the cooler object	This usually plays only a small part in temperature regulation, but we can all feel heat loss by conduction when taking some food from the freezer
Convection	Heat energy is transferred by particles moving and carrying the energy with them	When air or water vapour next to the body is warmed (by conduction), the particles move away from the body, carrying the heat energy with them; this is more pronounced if there is a wind — the 'wind-chill' factor
Radiation	Heat energy is lost by a body giving off electro-magnetic radiation; no particles are involved in the transfer	As activity increases, more warm blood flows to muscles and skin and the increased heat in the skin results in more heat loss by radiation — put your hand close to the face of someone 'flushed' after exercise and feel the radiant heat
Evaporation	When a liquid is converted into a vapour, heat energy is used	Water is vaporised in breathing and sweating and accounts for most of the heat loss in warm environments

The hypothalamus controls body temperature in mammals through the autonomic nervous system. It receives information about body temperature from two main sources:

- temperature sensors in the skin detect changes in the temperature of the skin and therefore indirectly detect changes in the environmental temperature
- sensors in the hypothalamus itself detect changes in the temperature of the blood flowing through it which reflects changes in the 'core' body temperature

The hypothalamus acts as a kind of body 'thermostat'. It monitors body temperature and compares the actual temperature against a 'pre-set' value (37°C in humans). Any significant deviation from this is detected and appropriate responses are initiated.

The responses to overheating are brought about by the 'heat loss' centre of the hypothalamus (in the anterior hypothalamus) while those to overcooling are brought about by the 'heat gain' centre (in the posterior hypothalamus).

The diagram below summarises the role of the hypothalamus in controlling body temperature.

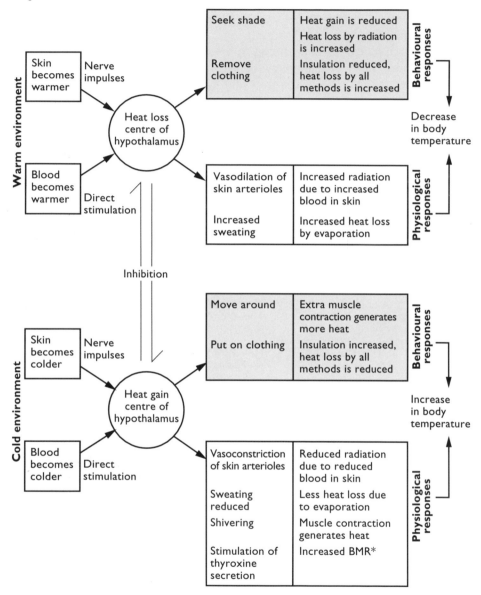

* Basal metabolic rate. This is the rate of energy expenditure when the person is awake but resting, has not eaten for 12 hours and is comfortably warm.

Controlling plasma glucose concentration

The islets of Langerhans in the pancreas contain two different types of secretory cell:

- α-cells, which secrete the hormone **glucagon**
- β-cells, which secrete the hormone **insulin**

The diagram below summarises the control of plasma glucose concentration by insulin and glucagon.

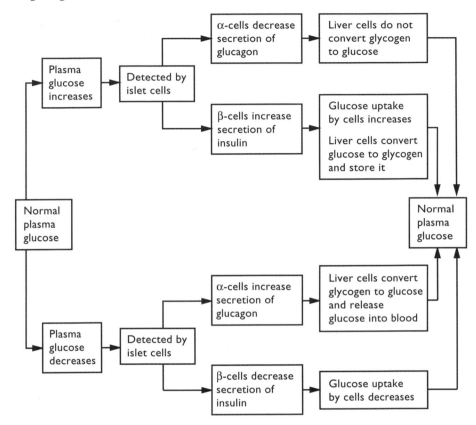

Both hormones bind to receptor proteins on the surface of liver cells and through a cascade system activate enzymes that catalyse the interconversion of glycogen and glucose. The diagram shows the cascade system that operates for insulin.

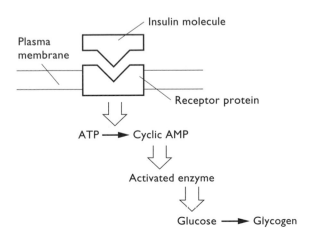

At each stage of the cascade, the effect is amplified. Each insulin molecule that binds to the receptor protein stimulates the formation of several molecules of cyclic AMP (called the **second messenger**), which in turn stimulates the activation of several enzyme molecules. Each enzyme molecule has a turnover rate of many thousands of glucose molecules per second.

The cascade system for glucagon is very similar, but the receptor is different and the cascade activates a different enzyme.

Tip Make sure you know the difference between **glucagon** and **glycogen**. The words are very similar — too similar for an examiner to make any allowance and give you the benefit of the doubt for any misspelling.

Plasma glucose concentration is also influenced by:
- adrenaline, which increases the release of glucose into the bloodstream (particularly during periods of stress or vigorous exercise)
- thyroxine, which increases BMR

Diabetes

Diabetes is a condition in which the islet β-cells are unable to secrete sufficient insulin. There are several causes of lack of insulin but, potentially, the danger is the same — a large intake of carbohydrate results in **hyperglycemia** (the plasma glucose concentration rises unchecked because cells cannot take up the glucose). As the level rises, there are several possible effects:
- the renal threshold is passed and glucose begins to appear in the urine (glucose cannot be reabsorbed fast enough in the nephrons of the kidney — see next section)
- because of the inability to reabsorb the glucose, large volumes of water are lost in the urine and the person constantly feels thirsty

Because the body cells cannot take up glucose, they metabolise lipids instead. This may result in the production of ketones which could lead to coma and death. Over a period of time, increased lipid metabolism can lead to more fatty substances circulating in the blood, causing an increased risk of atherosclerosis.

Diabetes can be controlled by:
- controlling carbohydrate intake
- injections of insulin

Controlling plasma water potential

The hypothalamus controls plasma water potential. Its main effect is on the posterior pituitary gland. It either stimulates it to secrete ADH (antidiuretic hormone) or inhibits this secretion. ADH acts on the walls of the collecting ducts in the kidney, increasing their permeability to water. More water is reabsorbed from the urine and less is lost. In the absence of ADH, the walls of the collecting ducts are less permeable to water and so more water is lost in the urine.

The role of the kidney in water balance is inextricably linked with the excretion of urea. The 'functional unit' of the kidney is the nephron.

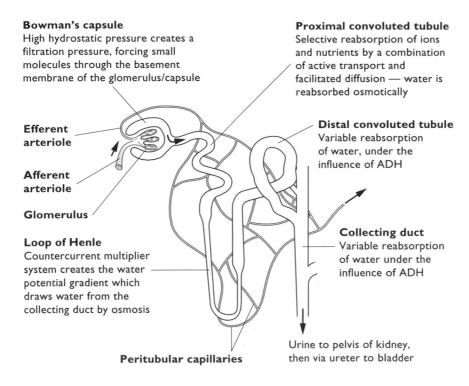

Bowman's capsule
High hydrostatic pressure creates a filtration pressure, forcing small molecules through the basement membrane of the glomerulus/capsule

Proximal convoluted tubule
Selective reabsorption of ions and nutrients by a combination of active transport and facilitated diffusion — water is reabsorbed osmotically

Efferent arteriole

Afferent arteriole

Glomerulus

Distal convoluted tubule
Variable reabsorption of water, under the influence of ADH

Loop of Henle
Countercurrent multiplier system creates the water potential gradient which draws water from the collecting duct by osmosis

Collecting duct
Variable reabsorption of water under the influence of ADH

Peritubular capillaries

Urine to pelvis of kidney, then via ureter to bladder

You should think of nephron function occurring in three main stages:

(1) Filtration in the glomerulus/Bowman's capsule
Any molecules small enough to cross the basement membrane are filtered from the blood into the capsule. Urea molecules are small enough but most protein molecules are too large.

(2) Reabsorption in the proximal tubule
Ions and nutrients are reabsorbed into the bloodstream by a combination of active transport and facilitated diffusion. There is no system to actively reabsorb urea but some diffuses back passively.

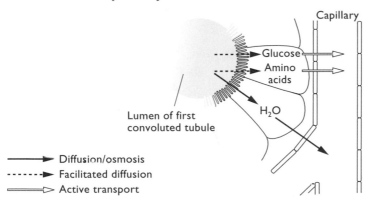

Capillary

Glucose

Amino acids

H_2O

Lumen of first convoluted tubule

⟶ Diffusion/osmosis
----▶ Facilitated diffusion
⟹ Active transport

(3) Reabsorption of water in the collecting ducts

The countercurrent multiplier system in the loop of Henle creates a concentration gradient in the medulla which results in the reabsorption of water from the collecting ducts, when ADH is present to make the walls permeable to water.

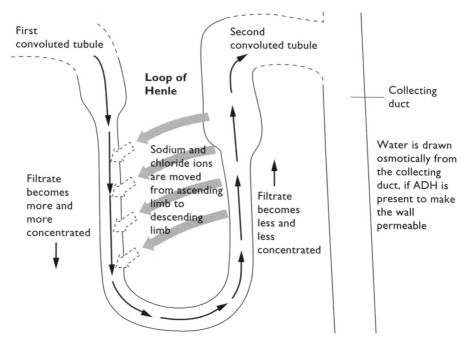

A gradient of concentration is set up such that, at any point, fluid in the tissue surrounding the collecting duct always has a more negative water potential (is more concentrated) than the collecting duct

⟶ Movement of filtrate

Nitrogenous excretory products

Urea is a 'nitrogenous excretory product'. It is formed from surplus amino acids (derived from surplus dietary proteins).

Not all animals convert surplus protein into urea: other excretory products include ammonia and uric acid. The liver **deaminates** amino acids, by removing the amino group to form a nitrogenous excretory product and a keto acid from the remainder of the molecule. Keto acids can then be respired, entering the respiratory chain at several points (see the Unit 5 guide for full details).

The nitrogenous excretory product formed is an adaptation to the habitat of the animal:

- Ammonia is highly toxic and must be eliminated from the body as soon as it is formed (or converted to something less toxic). Animals excreting ammonia excrete continuously and therefore lose water continuously. Fresh water fish gain water continuously by osmosis as it flows over the blood in their gills. They can 'afford' the water loss necessary to excrete ammonia.

- Urea is much less toxic than ammonia and can be stored for limited periods in the body before it is eliminated. However, its excretion still demands the loss of considerable amounts of water, which the animal must replace. Mammals can conserve water efficiently and so this method of excreting nitrogenous waste is effective.
- Uric acid is almost insoluble and is excreted as a paste with very little loss of water. It represents an adaptation to a terrestrial mode of life where water intake is restricted (e.g. reptiles in a desert).

What the examiners will expect you to be able to do

- Recall any of the key facts.
- Explain any of the key concepts.
- Interpret data on animal behaviour to identify the adaptive value of the behaviour and to identify the behaviour as a taxis or kinesis.
- Explain the benefits to a mammal of its homeostatic processes.
- Interpret data concerning changes in temperature, plasma glucose concentration and plasma water potential and explain the changes in terms of the control mechanisms that exist in the body of a mammal.
- Relate the habitat of an animal to its nitrogenous excretory product.
- Relate the structure of a mammalian nephron to its functions.
- Interpret data on changes in rate of urine flow and urine concentration linked to various environmental and dietary conditions (e.g. temperature, extra salt in the diet).

Synoptic links

Questions on homeostasis may contain sections on other related topics such as:
- biological molecules
- transport across membranes (osmosis, diffusion, facilitated diffusion, active transport)
- respiration
- transmission of nerve impulses
- control of heart beat by the sino-atrial node
- hydrolysis of proteins to amino acids

Questions
&
Answers

This section contains questions similar in style to those you can expect to see in your Unit 6 examination. The limited number of questions means that it is impossible to cover all the topics and all the question styles, but they should give you a flavour of what to expect. The responses that are shown are real students' answers to the questions.

The A2 unit tests are slightly different from the AS tests. There are still 75 marks in each test but the allocation of marks varies according to the style of question. You can expect the Unit 6 test to contain:

- six short-answer questions worth around 5 marks each, making a total of 30 marks (these will be similar in style to the short-answer questions you met in the AS unit tests)
- three longer questions, each worth 15 marks, comprising
  — two structured questions with a mixture of short-answer recall, data response and comprehension
  — one question that requires you to write in extended prose (there will be several parts, each requiring a 'mini-essay' type response)

Two thirds (50/75) of the marks will be for questions testing you directly on the Module 6 content. The rest (25/75) relate to some question sections that are **synoptic**. These test you on principles and concepts from other modules set in the context of the Module 6 content. For example, in a question on digestion, you may have to use the concepts of **condensation** and **hydrolysis**, which you learned in Module 1. In a question about transmission of nerve impulses across a synapse, you may have to use the concept of **unique tertiary structure of proteins** (again from Module 1) to explain why a neurotransmitter 'fits' its receptor.

There are several ways of using this section. You could:

- 'hide' the answers to each question and try the question yourself. It needn't be a memory test — use your notes to see if you can actually make all the points you ought to make
- check your answers against the candidates' responses and make an estimate of the likely standard of your response to each question
- check your answers against the examiner's comments to see if you can appreciate where you might have lost marks
- check your answers against the terms used in the question — did you *explain* when you were asked to, or did you merely *describe*?

Examiner's comments

All candidate responses are followed by examiner's comments. These are preceded by the icon *e* and indicate where credit is due. In the weaker answers, they also point out areas for improvement, specific problems and common errors such as lack of clarity, weak or non-existent development, irrelevance, misinterpretation of the question and mistaken meanings of terms.

uestion

Transport of respiratory gases

Oxygen is transported in mammalian blood by the protein haemoglobin in red blood cells. Figure 1 shows the dissociation curve for human haemoglobin at two different pHs.

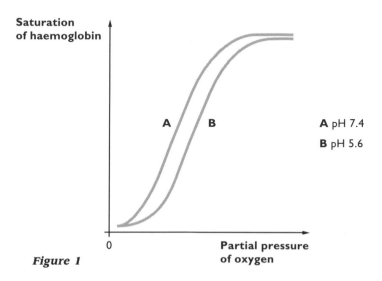

A pH 7.4

B pH 5.6

Figure 1

(a) Explain what is meant by 'the percentage saturation of haemoglobin'. (1 mark)

(b) Explain how vigorous exercise could produce a dissociation curve similar to that shown by line **B**. (2 marks)

(c) Explain how haemoglobin acts as a buffer. (2 marks)

Total: 5 marks

■ ■ ■

Candidates' answers to Question 1

Candidate A

(a) The amount of haemoglobin carrying oxygen.

Candidate B

(a) The percentage saturation of haemoglobin is the proportion of haemoglobin in a certain volume of blood that is actually carrying oxygen, that is, oxyhaemoglobin.

> ✎ Both candidates clearly understand the idea of saturation of haemoglobin, but in contrast to Candidate B, Candidate A has not answered precisely enough to score the mark. 'The amount of haemoglobin carrying oxygen' does not convey the idea of proportion. It could mean 10 g or 78 moles or *any other amount. Percentage* saturation must convey the idea of *proportion*; **the amount of haemoglobin bound to oxygen in 100 cm³ of blood** would be acceptable. **Read the question carefully**.

question

Candidate A

(b) Vigorous exercise would make the haemoglobin more acidic and so it would not carry oxygen as well. Curve B is lower than curve A.

Candidate B

(b) In vigorous exercise, a lot more carbon dioxide is released from the extra respiration. Carbon dioxide results in carbonic acid forming in the plasma, which will lower the pH of the plasma. Also, lactate (lactic acid) may be produced which would also lower the pH of the plasma. This change in the curve is called the Bohr effect or the Bohr shift.

> ✏ Candidate A does not really understand that the pHs referred to in the question are plasma pHs and cannot explain how vigorous exercise could change the pH. No marks are awarded. Candidate B gives a very full and clear explanation and is awarded both marks. **This synoptic question requires an understanding of the principles of respiration from Module 5.**

Candidate A

(c) Haemoglobin acts as a buffer by absorbing hydrogen ions to make the solution less acidic.

Candidate B

(c) Haemoglobin can bind with hydrogen ions and when it does, if it is already bound to oxygen, the oxygen is released. If the plasma becomes very acidic, there are a lot of hydrogen ions and so a lot of haemoglobin will bind to these hydrogen ions and make the plasma less acidic. This also means that more haemoglobin than usual will release oxygen to the surrounding tissues, which means that respiration can occur faster and release more energy.

> ✏ Candidate A just about has the idea that removing hydrogen ions from a solution (plasma would have been better) will increase the pH, but writing *absorbing* hydrogen ions makes it sound a little like a molecular sponge. Candidate B has given a full answer, but has then been distracted into writing about consequences relating to the efficiency of unloading oxygen, which are irrelevant to this question. **Don't waste time by giving unneeded explanations.** Candidate A is awarded 1 mark and Candidate B is awarded both marks.

> ✏ **Part (a) of this question is quite straightforward and a grade-C candidate should be able to answer it. Part (b) is synoptic and therefore requires you to make links with ideas from another module. Part (c) requires an understanding of the biochemistry of buffering and some quite difficult concepts. Grade-A candidates would be expected to understand these. Candidate A scores only 1 mark, while Candidate B scores 5.**

Water movement through a plant

Water can move across a plant root from the epidermis by the symplast pathway or the apoplast pathway until it reaches the endodermis. It can only move through the endodermis by the symplast pathway.

(a) (i) What is the symplast pathway? (1 mark)

(ii) Why can water not move through the endodermis by the apoplast pathway? (2 marks)

(b) Explain, in terms of water potential, why water moves across a plant root towards the endodermis. (2 marks)

Total: 5 marks

■ ■ ■

Candidates' answers to Question 2

Candidate A

(a) (i) Water moves through the cytoplasm in the symplast pathway, and not just through the cell walls.

Candidate B

(a) (i) The water crosses the cell wall and cell membrane into the cell and then moves through the cytoplasm and the vacuole before moving out again through the cell membrane and cell wall on the other side of the cell.

e Candidate A's answer is adequate, for 1 mark. Candidate B is also awarded the mark, but again has written more than necessary. **Take careful note of the mark allocation.**

Candidate A

(a) (ii) The cells of the endodermis have a layer called the Casparian strip in their cell walls, which stops water moving through.

Candidate B

(a) (ii) The endodermal cells have a layer of suberin in their cell walls (the Casparian strip) which is impermeable to water. As a result, water is diverted from the cell walls into the cytoplasm and must move through these cells by the symplast pathway.

e Candidate A only scores 1 of the 2 marks, as there is no explanation as to *why* the Casparian strip prevents the further movement of water. Candidate B has given this explanation, for both marks, but yet again has written more than necessary.

Candidate A

(b) The cells near the outside of the root have weaker solutions in them than those near the centre, so water moves by osmosis from the weaker cells to the stronger ones.

2

Candidate B

(b) There is a water potential gradient across the cortex and so water moves by osmosis along this gradient from the cells near the epidermis to the endodermis.

    e Neither candidate scores both marks. Candidate A has ignored the instruction to 'explain in terms of *water potential*'. The biology is correct, although an examiner would not be impressed reading about weak and strong cells. Candidate A is awarded 1 mark for involving osmosis and having the water move in the correct direction. Candidate B does not specify where the high water potential is and so only scores 1 mark. **This synoptic question requires an understanding of water potential from Module 1.**

    e **This would be considered a fairly straightforward question and both grade-A and grade-C candidates would be expected to score well. Candidate A scores 3 marks and Candidate B scores 4.**

question 3

Excreting nitrogenous waste

Figure 1 shows a cross-section through part of the first (proximal) convoluted tubule in a nephron of a mammal. Some processes involved in the reabsorption of substances into the bloodstream are also shown.

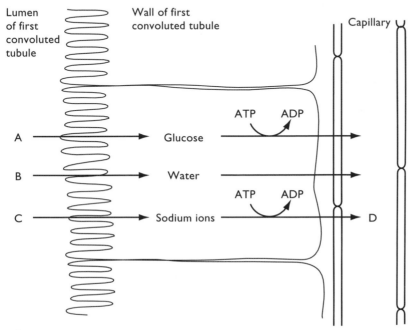

Figure 1

(a) Complete the table by placing a tick (✔) or cross (✗) in each box to indicate whether the feature applies or does not apply to each process.

Process	Feature of process		
	Substance moves against concentration gradient	Process is passive	Process requires carrier proteins
A			
B			
C			
D			

(3 marks)

(b) Explain why the presence of proteins in the urine might indicate damage to the glomeruli. (2 marks)

Total: 5 marks

■ ■ ■

Candidates' answers to Question 3

Candidate A

(a)

Process	Feature of process		
	Substance moves against concentration gradient	Process is passive	Process requires carrier proteins
A	✗	✔	✗
B	✗	✔	✗
C	✗	✔	✗
D	✔	✗	✔

Candidate B

(a)

Process	Feature of process		
	Substance moves against concentration gradient	Process is passive	Process requires carrier proteins
A	✗	✔	✔
B	✗	✔	✗
C	✗	✔	✔
D	✔	✗	✔

ℯ There is 1 mark per correct column. Both score the mark for the first two columns, and candidate B scores the other mark as well. Candidate A clearly equates only active processes with protein carrier molecules. **This synoptic question requires an understanding of transport across boundaries from Module 1.**

Candidate A

(b) Protein molecules are usually too large to pass into the nephron.

Candidate B

(b) Protein molecules generally have a molecular mass of 68 000 or more and so aren't filtered at the glomerulus. They remain in the blood and don't appear in urine. Only smaller molecules are filtered, but then most of these are reabsorbed.

ℯ Neither candidate has really addressed the issue as to why the presence of proteins indicates *damage* to the glomeruli. Both explain that normally proteins aren't filtered, for 1 mark, but don't say how this might change if the glomeruli are damaged. Candidate B has again been sidetracked into writing about issues that are irrelevant to the question (the fate of the smaller molecules). **Make sure you stay on task.**

ℯ **The question would not be a favourite of many candidates, but you should have no real problems if you revise not just the Module 6 content but also that of the other modules. Pay particular attention to those topics indicated earlier. Candidate A is awarded 3 marks, while Candidate B scores 4.**

Control of digestion and absorption of products

Digestion of proteins in the stomach of a mammal is under both nervous and hormonal control. These control mechanisms are summarised in the table.

Control mechanism	Stimulus	Response
Simple reflex arc (vagus nerve directly affects stomach)	Sight, smell and taste of food, distension of the stomach	Secretion of gastric juice, secretion of gastrin
Gastrin secretion (by stomach)	Impulses from vagus, distension of stomach	Stimulates secretion of gastric juice
Secretin secretion (by duodenum)	Presence of acid chyme released from the stomach	Inhibits secretion of gastrin

(a) Explain the value of:
   (i) the reflex control of secretion of gastric juice   (2 marks)
   (ii) the inhibition of gastrin secretion by secretin   (1 mark)
(b) Individual fatty acid molecules can diffuse freely through the cell membranes of epithelial cells in the ileum. Use your knowledge of membrane structure to explain why.   (2 marks)

Total: 5 marks

■ ■ ■

Candidates' answers to Question 4

Candidate A
(a) (i) As soon as you see or smell food you will produce gastric juice in your stomach so that by the time you have swallowed the food, the enzymes are in your stomach ready to digest it.

Candidate B
(a) (i) It coordinates the release of gastric juice (pepsin and hydrochloric acid) into the stomach. It would be wasteful to put energy into synthesising and releasing enzymes when the food is not there.

   e Candidate A makes both points required in the answer — just (2 marks). The reflex action is a quick response, which allows the secretion of gastric juice prior to food entering the stomach — anticipating the body's needs. Candidate B does not explain these points clearly enough and fails to score.

Candidate A
(a) (ii) Secretin stops the secretion of gastric juice when food leaves the stomach.

question

Candidate B

(a) (ii) Secretin is produced when food is leaving the stomach and so gastric juice secretion is no longer necessary. Secretin stops this secretion and so prevents the body wasting energy on synthesising enzymes when the food is not there.

e Both candidates are awarded the mark.

Candidate A

(b) Fatty acids are small molecules and so can diffuse freely through the phospholipid bilayer.

Candidate B

(b) The plasma membrane is made from a phospholipid bilayer and proteins. The bilayer decides what can pass freely through the membrane. Fatty acids are insoluble in the phospholipids and so pass through easily.

e Both candidates score 1 mark for demonstrating knowledge of the structure of a plasma membrane. Candidate B would have scored full marks if it wasn't for the unfortunate slip of writing 'insoluble' (instead of soluble). This synoptic question requires an understanding of plasma membranes and the passage of substances (Module 1).

e **The question is quite difficult since it requires you to combine ideas from several areas of the specification. In (a) (i) you must appreciate the importance of the speed and timing of the reflex control as well as the role of gastric juice in digestion. In part (b) you have to relate membrane structure to absorption. Examiners would understand a grade-C candidate having problems with this question, although Candidate A answers it well, for 4 marks, whereas Candidate B, the stronger candidate, gets sidetracked and scores just 2 marks.**

Hormone action

The level of plasma glucose at rest is largely maintained by the hormones insulin and glucagon. These are both secreted by islet cells in the pancreas and affect mainly skeletal muscle cells and liver cells.

(a) Explain why the hormones affect mainly skeletal muscle cells and liver cells.   (2 marks)

(b) Explain how one molecule of glucagon can bring about the conversion of many molecules of glycogen to glucose.   (2 marks)

(c) Name one other hormone that can influence the level of plasma glucose.   (1 mark)

Total: 5 marks

■ ■ ■

Candidates' answers to Question 5

Candidate A

(a) Liver and skeletal muscle cells are the target cells for insulin and glucagon so they bind to these cells in particular.

Candidate B

(a) Insulin and glucagon bind to protein receptors in the plasma membranes of these cells. The protein receptors are shaped so that only these hormones will fit — other cells don't have the same receptors.

> ℮ Candidate A uses the idea of binding but does not say to what, and does not explain why these cells are the target cells (0 marks). Candidate B makes both of these points, for full marks. **You need an appreciation of shape of protein receptor molecules from Module 1 to answer this synoptic question.**

Candidate A

(b) The hormone causes the cell to break down many molecules of glycogen, one after the other.

Candidate B

(b) When one molecule of glucagon binds, it activates an enzyme which catalyses the reaction of glycogen to glucose. An enzyme can catalyse the breakdown of many molecules of glycogen. As soon as one leaves the active site of the enzyme, another one can enter to be broken down. This is the turnover rate of the enzyme.

> ℮ Candidate A does not really present any information that was not already given in the question, and so scores no marks. **Beware of simply re-wording the question.** Candidate B clearly understands the cascade principle of hormone action, and is awarded 2 marks.

Candidate A

(c) Adrenaline

Candidate B

(c) Thyroxine increases the basal metabolic rate (BMR), increasing the rate at which glucose is used up.

e Both candidates are awarded 1 mark.

e **The question is not just about the effects of hormones. It is about how they bring about their effects and, as such, requires understanding of several areas of the specification. Candidate A should have been able to do better than 1 mark: the first section concerning targeting specific cells is straightforward if you understand the concept of specific receptor proteins. Candidate B scores full marks.**

Q6

Action potentials

Nerve impulses are propagated along the axons of neurones as a series of action potentials. Figure 1 shows the changes in membrane potential, sodium ion (Na^+) conductance and potassium ion (K^+) conductance of an axon membrane as an action potential is generated.

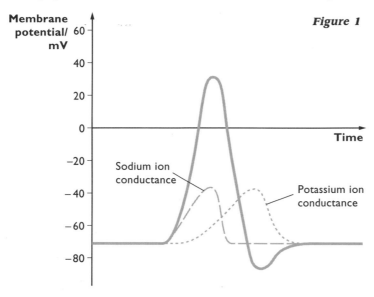

Figure 1

(a) Describe the evidence in the graphs that suggests that depolarisation is caused by an influx of sodium ions, while repolarisation is caused largely by the exit of potassium ions. (3 marks)

(b) Explain the role of the refractory period in the transmission of nerve impulses. (2 marks)

Total: 5 marks

■ ■ ■

Candidates' answers to Question 6

Candidate A

(a) The increase in the membrane potential happens at the same time as the increase in sodium conductance. This is when the action potential occurs, so it must be due to the sodium ions. When the membrane potential falls back to normal again, this corresponds with an increase in potassium conductance.

Candidate B

(a) The action potential is generated when the membrane potential becomes positive on the inside (it is usually 70 mV negative). The graph shows that this happens when the conductance to sodium ions increases, allowing these ions to rush in. To restore the membrane potential back to the 70 mV negative, potassium ions rush out. This can only happen when the membrane becomes permeable to potassium, which is shown by the increase in potassium ion conductance, after the peak occurs.

> Neither candidate has related the evidence to the terms 'depolarisation' and 'repolarisation'. Candidate A has described all the appropriate features in the graph, but has not related them to the terms 'depolarisation' and 'repolarisation' or related the evidence to the *events* of 'depolarisation' and 'repolarisation'. It is not at all clear that the candidate understands what these terms mean. Candidate B has not actually used the terms 'depolarisation' and 'repolarisation' but has described the *events* that are defined by the terms and has related the evidence to them. Candidate A scores 1 mark and Candidate B, 2 marks. **If you are asked to relate evidence to named events/processes, you will only score full marks if you can show that you understand these terms.**

Candidate A

(b) The refractory period is the period when an axon cannot have an action potential. This is because it becomes permeable to sodium ions and can't let them pass through.

Candidate B

(b) This is the time when the membrane is impermeable to the sodium and potassium ions, which means that a new action potential cannot be generated.

> Neither candidate has really got to grips with this; both score just 1 mark for the idea that an action potential cannot be generated. Candidate A comes closest to the second mark, but makes contradictory statements by saying that the membrane 'becomes permeable to sodium ions' and 'can't let them pass through'. **The examiner will not choose which of two contradictory statements a candidate really means: if the answer is not clear, it is wrong**. Even without this, the answer is still not quite correct. During the refractory period it is not just that the membrane is impermeable (not strictly true, anyway) but also that it *cannot easily become permeable* to the ions. This is a subtle, but important, distinction.

> **This is a topic that many candidates find difficult. You must be quite clear about what graphs like this one show, such as the changes in polarity of the *inside* of the axon, compared with the *outside*. Also, you need to understand that making the *inside* more *positive* requires *positive* ions (sodium ions — Na^+) to *enter*. Making the inside more negative again requires *positive* ions (potassium ions — K^+) to *leave*. Notice that negative ions are not involved. Candidate A scores 2 marks, while Candidate B score 3.**

Q7 uestion

Receptors and transmission of information through the nervous system

Sense cells, such as Pacinian corpuscles in the skin and rods and cones in the eye, are biological energy transducers. They transduce one form of energy from the environment into the electrochemical energy of a generator potential and an action potential. Nerve impulses may travel along neurones and across synapses to produce responses or they may be inhibited by action potentials from other neurones.

(a) Figure 1 shows the apparatus used in an investigation into the mode of action of Pacinian corpuscles. Figure 2 summarises the results obtained.

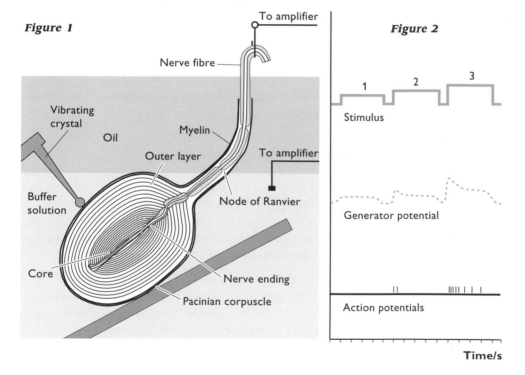

(i) How does the Pacinian corpuscle convert the vibrations of the crystal into a generator potential? (3 marks)

(ii) Suggest how the variations in the stimulus shown in Figure 2 could be generated using the above equipment. (2 marks)

(iii) Use your knowledge of the nature of nerve impulses to explain the results obtained. (3 marks)

(b) Figure 3 and the table beneath it show how several sensory neurones can influence a single motor neurone.

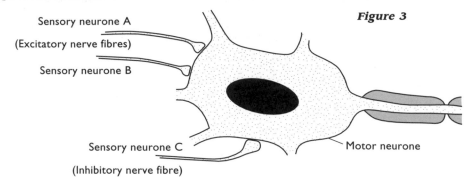

Sensory neurone A

(Excitatory nerve fibres)

Sensory neurone B

Figure 3

Sensory neurone C

(Inhibitory nerve fibre)

Motor neurone

Neurone	Action potential				
Sensory neurone A (excitatory)	✘	✔	✘	✔	✔
Sensory neurone B (excitatory)	✘	✘	✔	✔	✔
Sensory neurone C (inhibitory)	✘	✘	✘	✘	✔
Motor neurone	✘	✘	✘	✔	✘

(i) Explain why a nerve impulse can only cross a synapse in one direction. (4 marks)

(ii) Explain the results shown in the table. (3 marks)

Total: 15 marks

■ ■ ■

Candidates' answers to Question 7

Candidate A

(a) (i) The vibrations of the crystal squash the Pacinian corpuscle and the pressure causes the nerve ending to let ions in and out.

Candidate B

(a) (i) The pressure of the crystal is transmitted through to the core of the Pacinian corpuscle where it affects the permeability of the membrane. Pressure-sensitive sodium ion channels are opened and sodium ions enter to create a generator potential.

> *e* Candidate A has understood all the basic ideas about how a Pacinian corpuscle functions, yet manages to score no marks. The answer is simply too vague. Compare this with the same ideas expressed in much more detail and with no ambiguity in Candidate B's answer (full marks). **You must revise in detail**.

Candidate A

(a) (ii) The crystal vibrates and the oil will absorb some of the energy of the vibration. If you used less oil, the vibrations would be bigger.

Candidate B

(a) (ii) One could apply a larger voltage to make the crystal vibrate more.

> *e* Both candidates make sensible suggestions, but Candidate A's answer is *explained* in more detail, for full marks. Candidate B scores just 1 mark.

Candidate A

(a) (iii) When the stimulus gets larger, the generator potential also gets bigger and you get more action potentials. This is because the action potential can't get bigger — it's all-or-nothing.

Candidate B

(a) (iii) With more stimulation, the increased pressure opens more sodium ion channels and the generator potential is increased. Because the generator potential generates the action potential, there ought to be a bigger action potential as well. But action potentials are 'all-or-nothing' and so, instead of getting a bigger action potential, you get more action potentials.

> *e* Candidate B demonstrates a clear understanding of the situation and scores all 3 marks. Candidate A *describes* the relationship between stimulus, generator potential and action potential, but only *explains* why an increase in the generator potential does not produce an increase in the action potential, and so scores only 1 mark. **Make sure you *explain* what you are asked to explain.**

Candidate A

(b) (i) The ends of the pre-synaptic neurones contain vesicles of neurotransmitter. When an action potential reaches the end, these vesicles release their neurotransmitter and it diffuse across to the post-synaptic membrane. It can only pass one way because of the concentration gradient.

Candidate B

(b) (i) The synaptic knobs of the presynaptic neurone contain vesicles that produce the neurotransmitter. When an action potential arrives at the synaptic knobs, calcium ions enter and cause the vesicles to move to the surface and release their neurotransmitter into the synaptic cleft. It crosses the synaptic cleft and binds to protein receptor molecules on the post-synaptic neurone. This causes an action potential to be generated here and the nerve impulse is transmitted along the second neurone.

> *e* Candidate A scores 2 of the 4 marks, explaining how neurotransmitters cross the synaptic cleft (by diffusion) and why they pass in the direction they do (because of the concentration gradient). Candidate B gives a full account of how synaptic transmission takes place, but quite simply has not answered the question asked and so scores no marks. The issue is why the neurotransmitter *only* crosses the synapse in *one direction*. To score full marks, four of the following points must be made:
> - Only the pre-synaptic neurone has vesicles that produce the neurotransmitter.
> - Neurotransmitter diffuses across the synaptic cleft from the pre-synaptic membrane to the post-synaptic membrane.

- It diffuses in this direction because of the concentration gradient (higher near the pre-synaptic neurone).
- Binding to the receptor protein on the post-synaptic membrane removes transmitter from the cleft and maintains the gradient.
- The neurotransmitter is hydrolysed before being released by the post-synaptic membrane back into the synaptic cleft.

All the information about action potentials arriving and calcium ions entering is not really relevant to this question. **Make sure you read the question carefully and understand what is being asked. Don't go into unnecessary detail or get sidetracked into irrelevancies.**

Candidate A

(b) (ii) When several neurones act independently like this on another neurone, the effect is called summation. You only get an action potential in the motor neurone when A and B act together. If A and B act alone, or with C, there is no action potential in the motor neurone.

Candidate B

(b) (ii) Neurones A or B do not cause an action potential in the motor neurone on their own because they do not release enough neurotransmitter and so the threshold is not reached. When both have an impulse and both release neuro-transmitter, their combined effect is enough to pass the threshold and start an action potential. When either A or B or both A and B have an impulse with C, the inhibitory effect of C is enough to counteract A and B — together or separately. This is called summation.

e Neither candidate has explained *summation* satisfactorily. Candidate A has suggested that it occurs when neurones act *independently* — probably a slip as in the next line the neurones are described as acting together. The rest of Candidate A's answer is again a *description* of the results, not an *explanation*. No marks are awarded. Candidate B explains why A and B separately do not produce action potentials and why, together, they do. However, the answer does not *explain* the inhibitory effect of neurone C. Candidate B scores 2 marks. **Be clear about what the question is asking.** An examiner would look for the following points:

- Neurons A and B independently produce sub-threshold stimulation.
- Together, A and B exceed the threshold.
- This is called summation.
- Neurone C can prevent A and/or B exceeding the threshold.

e **The question demands a detailed understanding of Pacinian corpuscles and how transmission of nerve impulses takes place. You need to revise the material carefully and in detail. Candidate A could quite easily have scored 4 or 5 more marks here if more detail had been supplied. The answers appear to show *understanding*, but there is a lack of detail. There is no short cut to this and, equally, no magic — you must simply put the time in. Candidate A scores 5 marks and Candidate B, 9.**

Digestion and the excretion of nitrogenous waste

The flow chart shows how protein in the diet can be used to synthesise body proteins or be used in respiration.

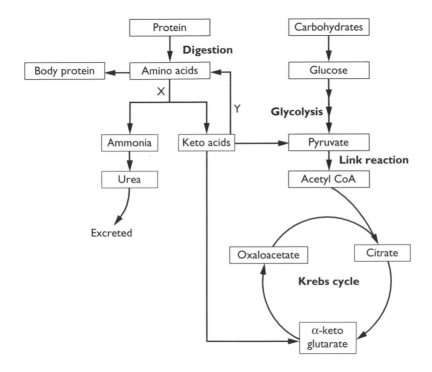

(a) (i) Name the processes labelled **X** and **Y**. (2 marks)

    (ii) Use the flow chart to explain why carnivorous mammals (such as wolves) do not need to eat much carbohydrate in their diet. (3 marks)

(b) (i) Explain how the peptide bonds in a protein molecule are broken during digestion. (3 marks)

    (ii) During the digestion of proteins in mammals, the molecules are first acted on by endopeptidases and then, later, by exopeptidases. Explain the advantage of the different enzymes acting in this order. (2 marks)

(c) Explain why freshwater fish excrete ammonia while mammals excrete urea. (5 marks)

Total: 15 marks

■ ■ ■

Candidates' answers to Question 8

Candidate A

(a) (i) X — deamination; Y — transamination

Candidate B

(a) (i) Process X is deamination (the amino group is removed from the amino acid). Process Y is transamination (the amino group is transferred from an amino acid to a keto acid — the keto acid becomes an amino acid and vice versa).

> *e* Both candidates score 2 marks, but why has candidate B again felt the urge to write far more than was necessary? If you are asked simply to name, then do just that. **You haven't the luxury of spare time in an examination to write more than is necessary.**

Candidate A

(a) (ii) Carnivores eat a lot of meat, which contains a lot of protein. This can be digested to amino acids, which can then be turned into keto acids and used in respiration in the Krebs cycle.

Candidate B

(a) (ii) The protein they eat can be digested and then deaminated, forming keto acids. These can then enter the respiratory chain after glycolysis. Glycolysis doesn't produce much energy and so there is little lost by not eating carbohydrate.

> *e* Both candidates score 2 of the 3 marks. Neither clearly makes the point that carbohydrate is a respiratory substrate, although both describe how protein can be processed for use as a respiratory substrate. Candidate B writes about glycolysis 'producing energy'. Try not to do this — it is impossible. Respiration (including glycolysis) releases energy and uses it to produce ATP. **Try to use language correctly — this is very important!**

Candidate A

(b) (i) Digestive enzymes like trypsin break down proteins by hydrolysis.

Candidate B

(b) (i) The peptide bonds are hydrolysed. A molecule of water is added across each peptide link (–NH–C=O) to break the bond, leaving amino (–NH$_2$) and carboxyl (–COOH) groups.

> *e* Both candidates understand that hydrolysis is involved. Candidate A has, unfortunately, drawn a diagram of condensation and so only scores 1 mark. Candidate B makes the point that water breaks bonds, for a second mark, but does not make

it clear *where* the amino and carboxyl groups are. A diagram would have helped here. Diagrams can often save you time and earn you marks. Be clear about what you are trying to show and make it accurate, but keep it as simple as possible. You must understand hydrolysis and the structure of protein molecules from Module 1 to answer this synoptic question.

Candidate A

(b) (ii) Exopeptidases act on the ends of protein molecules and endopeptidases on the middles. When the endopeptidases act on the proteins they make 'more ends' for the exopeptidases to act on and so digestion is faster.

Candidate B

(b) (ii) When the endo- ones have worked, there will be more terminal sequences for the exo- ones to act on. Digestion will be more effective.

e Both candidates clearly understand and score full marks.

Candidate A

(c) Mammals excrete urea because it is less toxic than ammonia and needs less water to get rid of it. Fish gain water all the time and so can excrete all the time. Therefore, they can excrete ammonia.

Candidate B

(c) Ammonia is very soluble and highly toxic. It cannot be stored in the body so it must be continually excreted. Freshwater fish must lose water all the time because they keep gaining it at the gills by osmosis, therefore they can excrete ammonia easily. Mammals have to conserve water, and can't excrete all the time, so they convert ammonia into urea, which is less toxic.

e Candidate A scores 3 marks for an answer that shows understanding but, as on several other occasions, lacks some detail. Candidate B gives a very detailed answer and scores all 5 marks.

e **None of the ideas in this question is very demanding, and both candidates score well (10 marks and 13 marks to A and B respectively). Again, however, Candidate A could have scored another 3 or 4 marks with more care and a little more preparation.**

Question 9

Controlling water loss in animals

Kangaroo rats (*Dipodymis spectabilis*) are able to survive in the desert without dinking any water. **Figure 1** shows the water losses and gains of the kangaroo rat at zero relative humidity (completely dry air) and a temperature of 25°C when fed only dry barley seeds. **Figure 2** shows the losses and gains at a relative humidity of 75% at 25°C when fed the same diet. The daytime temperatures in the desert are often greater than 35°C and the relative humidity is close to zero. As a consequence, kangaroo rats spend much of the day in underground burrows where the temperature range is 21–30°C and the humidity range is 30–50%. At night, when the desert temperature ranges from 15–22°C and the humidity ranges from 15–40%, they forage for food.

Figure 1   *Figure 2*

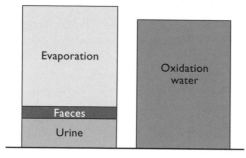

Zero humidity, 25°C

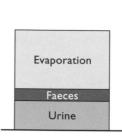

75% relative humidity, 25°C

(a) Explain the role of the hypothalamus and pituitary gland in keeping water losses in the kangaroo rat's urine to a minimum. (5 marks)

(b) Use the information to explain the adaptive behaviour of remaining in underground burrows during the daytime. (5 marks)

(c) The carbohydrate in the dried barley seeds was oxidised to produce 'metabolic water'. Explain why the amount of water used to digest a molecule of starch is less than that produced from its oxidation. (5 marks)

Total: 15 marks

■ ■ ■

Candidates' answers to Question 9

Candidate A

(a) The hypothalamus makes ADH, which affects how much water is lost in the urine. When the pituitary gland detects that the body is short of water, the hypothalamus releases ADH, which travels in the blood to the kidney. In the kidney, it causes more water to be absorbed by osmosis and so less is lost in the urine. This helps the kangaroo rat to conserve water.

Candidate B

(a) The hypothalamus makes ADH, but it is stored in the pituitary gland. Special receptors in the hypothalamus detect when the body is short of water and the hypothalamus 'instructs' the pituitary to release ADH. In the kidney, ADH causes the collecting ducts to become more permeable to water and so more is reabsorbed.

> *e* Candidate A has a basic understanding of the process and scores 3 marks. However, there is confusion about where the osmoreceptors are located and how ADH is stored and released. Also, there is no detail about where ADH acts in the kidney. Candidate B does not mention osmosis, but still gives an answer that merits full marks.

Candidate A

(b) Even at 25°C, in zero humidity, they lose so much water by evaporation that they lose more than they gain from all sources. If they went out in the desert at 35°C, this would be even worse and they would die. In the burrows, it's hot but humid and they lose less by evaporation and actually absorb some water. So they gain more than they lose. When they go out at night, it's cool and quite humid so they can survive because they gain more water than they lose.

Candidate B

(b) If they came out in the day, they would lose lots of water by evaporation because of the zero humidity. This would be made worse because the temperature in the desert is even higher than in the experiment. In the burrows, the level of humidity will actually mean that they can absorb some water.

> *e* Both candidates clearly understand the situation and have analysed the information in some detail. For once, however, it is Candidate A who supplies most detail and is awarded all 5 marks, while Candidate B scores 4.

Candidate A

(c) Water is used to digest starch to glucose. The glucose molecules are then respired to produce energy. But they produce carbon dioxide and water as well. More water is produced by respiration than is used by digestion, so the animal has a source of metabolic water.

Candidate B

(c) Oxidation of starch produces carbon dioxide and water during respiration. The starch would have to be digested to glucose; each bond broken would take one molecule of water, and so however many glucoses there were in the starch molecule, there would be one less water molecule used. Roughly, though, each molecule of glucose formed will use up one molecule of water. The equation for respiration is:

$$C_6H_{12}O_6 + 6O_2 \longrightarrow 6CO_2 + 6H_2O + \text{energy released}$$

So each molecule of glucose respired produces six molecules of water — that is a 'profit' of five molecules of water.

Candidate A appreciates, in principle, why more water is produced during oxidation than is used during hydrolysis but, when compared with Candidate B's answer, detail is once again lacking. Candidate A scores 2 marks and Candidate B scores 4. Neither candidate mentions that **digestion takes place by hydrolysis. This synoptic question requires an understanding of both hydrolysis (Module 1) and respiration (Module 5).**

Both candidates have scored well on the question (Candidate B very well). It is often a topic that produces answers with a lot of detail about biology not directly related to the question. In this case, both candidates have been careful to relate their answers to the situations given.

Examiner's overview

There are 75 marks available in these nine questions, just as there will be in your test. They are intended to be representative of the sort of mix of questions you can expect.

Candidate B scores 58 of the 75 marks available — enough for a grade **A.** Candidate A scores 39 of the 75 marks and would be awarded a grade C. There are two important points about this candidate's work.

(1) The candidate does not perform evenly throughout the test: some questions are answered well, others poorly. For example, there were only 9 marks out of 30 awarded for questions 1, 5, 6 and 7; if the rest of the paper had been of this standard, Candidate A would only just have been awarded a grade E. However, 24 marks out of 35 were scored on questions 4, 8 and 9, which is representative of grade-A work. This inconsistency is in part due to gaps in knowledge and understanding but also to a lack of preparation.

(2) There are several occasions on which Candidate A makes statements which a little thought would have shown to be inappropriate:

- In question 1(a), the candidate describes a percentage as an amount — percentage must convey the idea of proportion (1 mark lost).
- In question 2(b), although the movement of water across the cortex of the root is clearly understood and explained, it is not *explained* in terms of *water potential*, as the question expressly asks (1 mark lost).
- In question 6(b), the candidate describes a membrane becoming *permeable* and being *unable to let ions pass*. You cannot expect a mark for statements that contradict one another (1 mark lost).
- In question 7(a)(i), the candidate states that a change in permeability of the Pacinian corpuscle membrane lets ions *in and out*. Which? (1 mark lost).
- In question 7(b)(ii), the candidate carelessly refers to summation as neurones acting *independently* (1 mark lost).

- In question 8(b)(i), the candidate carelessly draws condensation instead of hydrolysis: at this level you should know that any *lysis* involves splitting, not joining (2 marks lost).

If all of these careless and unnecessary mistakes had not been made, candidate A would have scored 46 out of the 75 marks available and would have been awarded a grade B.

In addition, there were three areas in particular where there was clearly no problem with understanding the concept involved in the question, but a lack of detail lost several marks:

- In question 7(a)(i), the candidate gives a sketchy account of how the Pacinian corpuscle functions, demonstrating understanding, but the lack of detail meant that no marks were scored.
- In question 8(c), the candidate shows clear understanding and some detail, but more detail was needed for a really good answer.
- In question 9(c), the candidate shows understanding of oxidation and hydrolysis but again the answer lacks detailed knowledge.

The candidate could probably have scored another 5 or 6 marks on these answers if the detail had been included. Perhaps just one more revision session would have enabled this. This could have taken the total to 51 or 52 out of 75, which would probably have been awarded a grade A.

Here we see a grade-C candidate who, with just a little more determination, could have been a grade-A candidate. There would have been no need to make quantum leaps in understanding, just more care in the examination and a little more time spent on revision. Will you be able to find that extra 2–3 hours?

Sodium./K^+ pump - uses energy to pumps out Na^+
4 pump in K^+ ions. (in2 cytoplasm)

At Resting pot^n $[K^+] = \uparrow$ inside $\downarrow$ outside.

$[Na^+] = \downarrow$ inside $\uparrow$ outside.

$[a-] = \downarrow$ inside $\uparrow$ outside.